ADVANCE PRAISE

"This book is medicine for the soul, bringing light to dark places. Author Tim Desmond offers deep insights from Buddhist psychology in the simplest of terms, inviting readers to explore brief practices that feel just right for them. In these pages, wisdom and compassion are inseparable, the fruit of the author's own sincere practice under the guidance of Zen master Thich Nhat Hanh. If you want to rekindle a spark that seems lost forever, this gentle, inspiring book is a trustworthy guide."

—**Christopher Germer, PhD**, lecturer, Harvard Medical School, author of *Mindful Path to Self-Compassion*, and codeveloper of the Mindful Self-Compassion program

"Anyone who has been depressed knows it can be a relentless, isolating weight—one that drains color, meaning, and hope from life. In *Buddhist Practices for Overcoming Depression*, Tim Desmond weaves together ancient Buddhist wisdom and contemporary psychology to offer a clear, compassionate way to meet even the heaviest moods with mindful presence and self-kindness. Through simple, grounded practices, he helps readers rediscover moments of connection, warmth, and vitality. For those caught in depression's grip, this book offers something rare and essential: trustworthy guidance on the path back to aliveness."

—**Tara Brach**, author of *Radical Acceptance* and *Radical Compassion*

BUDDHIST PRACTICES *for* OVERCOMING DEPRESSION

BUDDHIST PRACTICES *for* OVERCOMING DEPRESSION

Tim Desmond

Norton Professional Books

An Imprint of W. W. Norton & Company
Independent Publishers Since 1923

Note to readers: *Buddhist Practices for Overcoming Depression* is intended to provide general information on the subject of health and well-being; it is not a substitute for medical or psychological treatment and may not be relied upon for purposes of diagnosing or treating any illness. Please seek out the care of a professional health care provider if you are pregnant, nursing, or experiencing symptoms of any potentially serious condition. As of press time, the URLs displayed in this book link or refer to existing sites. The publisher and author are not responsible for any content that appears on third-party websites.

Printed in the United States of America
First Edition

For information about special discounts for bulk purchases, please contact W. W. Norton Special Sales at specialsales@wwnorton.com or 800-233-4830

Manufacturing by Versa Press
Book design by Anna Knighton
Production manager: Gwen Cullen

ISBN: 978-1-324-08245-3 (Paperback)

W. W. Norton & Company, Inc., 500 Fifth Avenue, New York, NY 10110
www.wwnorton.com
W. W. Norton & Company Ltd., 15 Carlisle Street, London W1D 3BS

Authorized EU representative: EAS, Mustamäe tee 50, 10621 Tallinn, Estonia

1 2 3 4 5 6 7 8 9 0

This book is dedicated to our spiritual ancestors who forged the path of healing, and to our descendants who we might make the world better for.

CONTENTS

SECTION III: TRANSFORMING OBSTACLES TO CHANGE

ACKNOWLEDGMENTS

Everything I've learned about how to transform suffering and cultivate joy in myself and others I have learned from Thich Nhat Hanh, the monks and nuns of Plum Village, and the other spiritual teachers I've been fortunate enough to meet. I can't thank them enough.

I also feel deep gratitude for the support and encouragement I've received from mentors and friends, especially Joanne Friday, Richie Davidson, Tara Brach, and Larry Boyang. Thank you to Johanna Hoffman for the inspiring conversations that helped clarify and organize these teachings.

All of the people at W. W. Norton have been incredibly helpful in bringing this book into existence. Thanks so much for your guidance and support in this project.

To my wonderful son Finnegan, thank you for being such an inspiration and source of love in the world.

INTRODUCTION

A BUDDHIST APPROACH TO OVERCOMING DEPRESSION

Poet and author Sylvia Plath described depression as feeling cut off from the world and numb, like living trapped under a glass jar. You can see the world and hear people laughing, but none of it touches you.

David Foster Wallace called depression an "invisible agony" and a "nausea of the soul." In his writing, he returns again and again to the experience of a kind of suffering that doesn't look dramatic but is instead numbing, flattening, and relentless.

Andrew Solomon writes that depression is "a slower way of being dead," a condition in which the world doesn't disappear but becomes unreachable.

I believe that anyone who's experienced depression can relate to these descriptions.

Depression is not merely a lot of sadness, although sadness can certainly be part of it. The lived experience of depression affects every aspect of our mind and body. Yet from within, it's extremely hard to see oneself clearly, and therefore to understand what's happening and why.

From a Buddhist perspective, depression can emerge in several different ways:

- It can start as a loss or trauma that changes our views (*micchā-diṭṭhi*) about ourselves or the world.

- It can come from a way of thinking (often modeled by our parents but not always) that amplifies the negative conditions in our lives and minimizes the positive (*ayoniso manasikāra*).
- It can come from the belief that being lovable or content requires something that we don't have or can't do (*bhava-taṇhā*).
- It can come from repeated experiences over time of being unable to take any action that makes life better, and eventually learning to stop trying (*akiriyā-diṭṭhi*).
- For a handful of people, it can come from a medical condition like the side effects of a medication or a thyroid imbalance.
- For a huge number of people with depression, there can be a deep (often hidden) part of oneself that seems to resist all attempts to change (*anusaya* or *vāsanā*).

Buddhism offers practices to transform all the different root causes of depression. However, since one person's depression can be very different from another's, the practices that resonate for you won't be the same as for everyone else. This book aims to make it as easy as possible to find the specific practices that resonate for you as an individual.

BUDDHIST PRACTICES *for* OVERCOMING DEPRESSION

SECTION I

FINDING *the* ENERGY *to* CHANGE

1

WHY BOTHER?

If you feel ready to begin training your mind, you can skip directly to Section II. If it's difficult to find the energy, then begin with this section.

Depression doesn't always feel like sadness. It can feel like a wall, or like numbness. It can feel like tightness in your chest or a weight behind your eyes. It can feel like dragging yourself through mud just to brush your teeth, or looking at your to-do list like it belongs to someone else's life. For many of us, no matter how depression shows up, there's a feeling inside that says, "Why bother?"

We might experience that feeling as hopelessness, bitterness, or a deep resignation. Sometimes it feels like "Nothing ever changes," or "Even if I try, it won't make a difference." Sometimes it comes out indirectly as resentment toward others or shame toward ourselves. Whatever form it takes, the energy behind "Why bother?" is one of powerlessness and withdrawal.

So let's start there. Let's start in the very real place where effort feels unreachable. Where part of you might not want to open this book.

That's okay.

This book is not here to make grandiose promises or tell you to try harder. It's here to walk *with* you as you are. Even if all you can muster is curiosity—*What if this could help?*—that's enough.

WHAT IS THE ENERGY BEHIND "WHY BOTHER?"

One way to understand the experience of depression is through the lens of energy conservation. When we're deeply depressed, our nervous system can shift into a state that resembles hibernation: slow, still, and low. In some situations, this could be adaptive for survival. If your efforts to improve your life have repeatedly failed or brought pain, at some point your mind will conclude: *Effort is dangerous. Hope is dangerous. Better to stay still and wait.*

That's not laziness. It's learning from experience.

The part of you that says, "Why bother?" might be trying to keep you safe from more disappointment, more shame, or more exhaustion. It could be protecting you the only way it knows how: by freezing.

Sadly, this protection ends up becoming a prison. Therefore, part of what we explore in this book is how to help that protective voice let go. Not by arguing with it. Not by force. But by *building a new model of the world* in which every part of your heart and mind trusts that you can take actions that make your life better.

"WHY BOTHER?" AS A BELIEF SYSTEM

If we look closer, "Why bother?" isn't just a feeling. It's a worldview. It's a set of beliefs about what's possible, what's worth it, and who we are.

Sometimes these beliefs sound like:

- "Nothing I do ever works."
- "Even if I feel better for a moment, it won't last."
- "Other people can change, but not me."
- "I don't deserve to be happy."

These beliefs are often unconscious, running in the background like operating systems. They feel so true because they seem to match our experience over and over again.

However, *they are still beliefs*, and beliefs can be questioned. They can be tested.

This book is an invitation into what the Buddhist tradition calls *verifying faith*. Not blind belief, not wishful thinking, but the willingness to test something with your own experience. To ask, "What happens when I try this practice? How does my mind feel when I do this meditation?"

Verifying faith is different from hoping for a miracle. It's the courage to experiment and see what's actually true for you—not based on what anyone else says, but based on your own felt experience.

That courage is the seed of something precious: the energy to change.

THE FIRST STEP IS NOT MOTIVATION, IT'S AWARENESS

Building motivation to change is important, but in my experience, *awareness comes first.*

Can you become aware of what "Why bother?" feels like in your body? Can you notice the tone of voice it speaks with inside you? Is it flat, angry, or scared?

Can you begin to see it not as *you*, but as a part of you? A part that might have learned something painful and is trying to keep you from being hurt again.

In Buddhist psychology, we often talk about parts of ourselves as seeds in the garden of the mind. There is a seed of despair in you. A seed of "Why bother?" that has been watered, probably for years. It might have been watered by your family, by trauma, or by your culture.

However, you are more than just that seed.

There are other seeds in you: of joy, curiosity, and kindness. They may be small. They may be buried deep, but they're there. Part of the work of this book is learning how to *water those seeds*, and how to embrace and care for the ones that hurt.

A SPIRIT OF EXPERIMENTATION

If this book has any request, it's not "try harder." It's "see for yourself."

There's a teaching of the Buddha called "The Better Way to Catch a Snake." He said that for every true teaching, there's always a way to pick it up from the wrong end. If you grab a snake by the tail, it will whip around and bite you. That doesn't mean snakes are bad, and it doesn't mean the teaching is wrong. It means you have to use your intelligence to work with it wisely.

See if you can bring that spirit to everything in this book.

None of these practices are magic. They can help you suffer less, but only if you apply them in a way that fits you. In order to do that, you'll have to experiment. If something doesn't feel right, you may have picked it up from the wrong end. That's not failure—it's a signal. Step back, reflect, and see if there's another way to understand the practice. Try again, gently, from another angle.

In ancient India, very small amounts of snake venom were used in powerful medicines. What was dangerous in one context became healing in another. The same is true for deep teachings. These practices can be transformative, but only when applied with awareness.

As you move through this book, keep checking in with your body and your heart. Ask yourself, "Does this feel nourishing? Does this support my healing?" If the answer is no, pause. See if there's a different way to relate to the practice that works better for you.

Let that be your guide. Not the pressure to follow directions exactly, but a wise, personal engagement with what's offered. That's how practice becomes your own.

If you feel ready, try this practice:

PRACTICE: A GENTLE LOOK AT "WHY BOTHER?"

- Find a quiet place to sit and take a few calming breaths.
- Bring to mind the part of you that feels like nothing matters. The part that says, "What's the point?"
- See if you can locate that feeling in your body. Is it heaviness? Tightness? Numbness?
- Breathe while you feel it.
- Say silently, "I see you. I know you're in pain, and you need love. I'm here with you." Don't try to change it. Just keep it company.
- After a few minutes, try saying, "However I'm feeling in this moment, I deserve love."

This is one way to begin a new relationship with your depression. Not as something to battle, but as something to understand.

A DOOR, NOT A WALL

The feeling of "Why bother?" might seem like a wall, but it can be a door. By offering loving-presence to that feeling, it can open, revealing the possibility that the world might not be exactly what your depression says it is.

Buddhism teaches that reality is always larger, more alive, and more dynamic than our thoughts about it. That even when we feel completely stuck, there are *infinite conditions*—some beautiful, some painful—happening right now.

You don't have to see them all. You don't have to force yourself to feel grateful or inspired. All you need is one drop of curiosity. *Is it possible that life has more in store for me than I've been able to see?*

That question can be the first step out of the dark.

2

CALLING A CEASEFIRE

It's easy to hate depression.

It makes us tired. It pulls us away from the people we care about. It interferes with our ability to work, to feel pleasure and hope. It can make us bitter, ashamed, impatient, or numb. It turns everyday life into something we have to survive, rather than something we can enjoy.

So when people talk about healing depression by being kind to it, it can sound like a bad joke.

My teacher, Thich Nhat Hanh, used to say we must hold our pain the way we would hold a crying baby. He said to bring it into our arms, breathe with it, and offer it our tenderness. That teaching has changed many lives, including mine. Yet I also know that for some of us, depression doesn't feel like a crying baby. It feels like a terrifying monster—something dangerous and overwhelming. Not something you want to cradle, but something you want to run away from.

That reaction makes sense. If your depression has made your life harder for a long time, it's completely reasonable to want to fight it, reject it, and push it away. However, fighting your depression takes energy. And when you're depressed, energy is already in short supply. The harder you fight, the more depleted you become. Since this fight is happening inside your own mind and body, you're the only one who gets hurt.

You can think of this as a type of inner war. One part of you is suffering, and another part of you is attacking it. You end up caught in a self-sustaining loop, hurting in response to hurting. Worst of all, if you recognize this dynamic inside yourself, you might be tempted to attack your habit of attacking your suffering. Please don't.

You've been trying to survive with the tools you have, and the time has come to call a ceasefire. A ceasefire is not a surrender. It's not a decision to let depression take over. A ceasefire is a pause in the fighting, which is long enough to see what's really happening.

Calling a ceasefire doesn't mean you stop caring about healing. It doesn't mean you stop trying to feel better. What it means is that you stop relating to your depression as an enemy. You stop imagining that attacking your pain is the same as healing it. Instead, you learn to see depression as a form of suffering. And suffering, in the Buddhist tradition, is something that needs to be understood, not punished. It always needs love, and often it needs guidance.

For most of us, this shift doesn't happen all at once. It begins slowly, in small moments. You notice yourself bracing, or pushing, or criticizing yourself for feeling the way you do. However, instead of following that momentum, you pause. You take one breath. You let go of the idea that you need to fix everything right now. Just for that moment, you choose not to fight.

That's the beginning of a new kind of relationship with yourself.

In the chapters that follow, we explore practices to build motivation, cultivate joy, and learn how to be present with what's hard. But none of that works very well if you're still at war with yourself. That's why we start here. We start with one quiet breath, and one decision to stop hurting yourself in the name of getting better.

You don't have to like your depression. You don't have to welcome it. But if you can stop fighting it—if you can see it as a form of pain, not a personal failure—you'll have more energy available for healing. That energy is what this first section is all about.

So just for today, see if you can lay down your weapons. Even if only for a breath or two.

PRACTICE: ONE MOMENT OF CEASEFIRE

This practice is meant to be accessible even when you feel depleted. Try it and see how you feel:

- Sit or lie down in any comfortable position.
- Close your eyes, or let your gaze rest on something neutral.
- Take one breath and say silently, "I don't have to fix anything right now."
- Take another breath and say, "I'm not at war with myself."
- Take one more breath and say, "My pain needs love, not punishment."

- Rest there for a few more breaths if you want. Notice how you feel.

You can repeat this practice anytime during the day—when you notice yourself struggling, when you feel shut down, or when you simply need a moment of peace.

It may not feel like much, but even a few breaths of nonviolence can make space for something new to emerge.

RESISTANCE IS PART OF THE PROCESS

It's normal to feel skeptical about this. You may wonder, *If I stop fighting my depression, won't I just give in to it*? That's a reasonable fear, especially if you've relied on internal pressure to keep yourself moving. However, pressure is not the same as motivation. Pressure wears us down. Motivation grows when we feel safe enough to take a step forward.

By calling a ceasefire, you create conditions where your depression can be seen and cared for, rather than feared or hated. And the nature of suffering is that it heals through receiving care.

This is not the same as passivity. It's not the same as resignation. It's the beginning of clarity.

YOU CAN COME BACK TO THIS

The ceasefire doesn't have to be permanent. You don't have to be perfectly peaceful toward yourself every moment of every day. Most people return to old patterns, and that's okay.

What matters is finding a way back. If you know what it feels like to pause, to soften, to stop the inner attack, and you know you can return to that space—even if just for a moment—then you have the beginning of a path out of the darkness.

In time, these moments can become a new habit. A default setting of patience rather than judgment. Curiosity rather than resistance. Not because you tried harder, but because you built a new kind of relationship with your pain.

WHAT COMES NEXT

If the practice of ceasefire feels like a relief, you might stay with it for a while. When you're ready, read the next few chapters slowly, and find your own way of relating to the ideas in them.

If the idea of calling a ceasefire brings up anxiety or fear, then skip to Section III. There are teachings and practices there to guide you through any resistance you feel. If not, just notice what shifts, even slightly, when you stop fighting yourself. That shift is your first glimpse of the energy you've been using to keep the war going. It's energy that can be reclaimed, gently, for healing.

You don't have to do everything at once. Just don't hurt yourself in the name of progress.

That's the ceasefire.

3

SADDHĀ: A BUDDHIST APPROACH TO FAITH

In Buddhism, the word *saddhā* is often translated as "confidence" or "faith." But it's not the kind of faith that asks you to believe something without evidence. Buddhist faith is never blind. It doesn't mean believing in something just because someone told you to. Instead, *saddhā* is a kind of deep trust in your own experience. Eventually, it's a trust in the possibility of transformation.

Faith in the possibility of change can be especially difficult to access when you're depressed. In fact, that difficulty is part of what depression is. Almost everyone experiencing depression carries, at some level, the belief that no action they take would make a meaningful difference. That belief might come from having tried and failed, or it might be a deep, unshakable sense that things will always feel this way. The suggestion that you should have confidence in change can feel threatening. It might provoke fear, exhaustion, or even disgust. This, too, is part of the trap. When you're certain your efforts won't matter, you don't try. Without trying, nothing improves. You can see how self-reinforcing this worldview can be.

The belief, however fragile, that something *could* shift is precisely what makes action possible. And taking action is what makes healing possible.

In the Buddhist path, *saddhā* is considered the first of the five powers—alongside energy, mindfulness, concentration, and insight. It's always listed first because in practice, it always precedes the others. No one would try to change unless some part of them believes that change is possible.

Faith here means believing that it's possible to have a life with less suffering and more freedom, connection, and joy. That there is a path forward, and that you are capable of walking it.

THREE KINDS OF FAITH

In traditional Buddhist psychology, *saddhā* is said to unfold in three stages. They aren't necessarily linear, and you might move back and forth among them. Each one has its own beauty and its own role to play in healing.

1. Bright Faith

Bright faith is when you hear something that moves you. Maybe it's a teaching, or maybe it's someone else's story of how they changed. It could just be the feeling that someone understands what you're going through. In that moment, something in you lights up. You think, "Maybe this could help me too."

This is the spark of possibility. It's not based on your own direct experience, but in a way, it's borrowed from another person's experience. You don't yet know for yourself that the path works—but someone else seems to, and you feel their confidence. This is called *bright faith*, and sometimes it's all we have at the beginning. If you're reading this book and finding something useful, maybe you're experiencing bright faith. You don't have to be sure. Just being open is enough.

Sometimes people tell me, "I don't know if I can believe that healing is possible for me." If that's where you are, maybe you can borrow some of *my faith*. In my own life, I've seen these practices work. When I began with these practices, I was in a deep hole of suffering. I was angry and lonely, carrying the pain of having grown up poor with a single, alcoholic mother. Over the course of my life, these practices have helped me find more love and joy than I would have thought possible. Now, in my work as a therapist and meditation teacher, I've seen countless people transform their lives as well. I believe in your capacity to change too.

2. Verifying Faith

Verifying faith is what happens when you're ready to try something for yourself. It doesn't require complete confidence, just enough openness to experiment. It's a humble kind of faith—the kind that says, "I don't know, but I'm willing to find out."

This kind of faith can be difficult when you're depressed, because trying something new often feels pointless or exhausting. However, it also can be empowering, because it doesn't require you to believe anything in particular. You just show up, practice, and observe.

Verifying faith is honest. It doesn't make grand claims. It just says, "I'm going to try this and see what happens."

3. Abiding Faith

Abiding faith arises from your own experience. It's what happens when you've tried the practices, you've seen the results, and you know in your bones that this path is real.

It's not about believing in a theory. It's about remembering the moments when you felt more whole, more awake, and more connected. Even if those moments were brief, they matter. They're yours, and no one can take them from you.

When abiding faith is present, you don't need to force yourself to practice. You're drawn to it because you've tasted its fruit. You've seen that healing is possible—not just in theory, but in your own life.

SADDHĀ AS THE WILLINGNESS TO BEGIN AGAIN

Sometimes we think of faith as a feeling we're supposed to have. However, in Buddhist practice, *saddhā* is more like a willingness to begin again. A willingness to say, "I don't know if this will work, but it could, so I'll try." Even if the feeling of hopelessness is there inside you, just showing up is an act of faith.

You don't need to manufacture belief. You don't need to feel inspired or convinced. Just practice. Take one breath. One step. One moment of kindness toward yourself.

Sometimes *saddhā* doesn't feel like grace—it feels like grit. Like a tired person who's still walking. And that kind of faith is holy too.

IF RESISTANCE ARISES

If you notice resistance coming up as you read this, that's not a problem. It's an expected part of the process. When you've been living with depression, even considering the idea of change can feel threatening. You may not fully believe in the possibility of healing, or you may believe in it in general, but not for you. That kind of resistance can show up as skepticism, numbness, defensiveness, or a sharp inner "no."

In this book, we call those kinds of blocks *inner obstacles*. They often take the form of a competing commitment—some part of you that has a hidden reason to resist change, even if it causes suffering. Maybe change feels unsafe. Maybe it feels disloyal. Maybe it just feels impossible. These are not signs of failure. They're signs that something deeper needs attention.

If you feel a strong sense of resistance to the ideas in this chapter, turn to Section III. That part of the book is designed specifically for working with inner obstacles. You don't have to push through resistance. In fact, trying to do that often backfires. Instead, we have to understand the nature of the resistance before it's possible to navigate a way through.

There's no need to move in a straight line. If you start to feel stuck, jump ahead. Come back when you're ready. Let the structure of this book serve your process, not the other way around.

CULTIVATING SADDHĀ

Try whispering to yourself:

"Healing might be possible."

"It could be hard, and I might not know how, but that doesn't mean it's impossible."

"It could be possible for me."

If that feels okay, go a step further and try:

"Healing is possible."

"It is possible for anyone if they find the right path for them."

"I don't know if this will be the right path for me, but it's worth trying."

That's *saddhā*. That's how healing begins.

4

VIRIYĀ: THE ENERGY THAT DRIVES PRACTICE

The second of the five powers in Buddhist psychology is *viriyā*. It's usually translated as "energy," "effort," or "diligence." In the context of healing, it might be better understood as motivation—the force that helps us take action in the direction of what matters.

This isn't the kind of energy that keeps us chasing one accomplishment after another without ever feeling whole. *Viriyā* is different. It's the kind of motivation that comes from clarity. It arises when we understand, even a little, what will genuinely lead to less suffering and more freedom. It's steady, grounded effort—effort that aligns with what truly matters. When you know which direction leads toward healing, *viriyā* is the part of you that's willing to take a step. Not because you're forcing it, but because you can see that the step is worth taking.

This is the part of Buddhism that can feel like a coach giving an inspirational speech. You feel that change is possible through *saddhā*. You feel that it's worth the effort through *viriyā*.

HOW TO CULTIVATE VIRIYĀ

In the classical teachings, *viriyā* is cultivated by reflecting on two things:

1. *The benefits of practice:* What your life could look and feel like if you were less caught in suffering.
2. *The dangers of not practicing:* What can happen if nothing changes.

Both reflections serve the same purpose: to help you remember that how you relate to your suffering matters. Your choices matter. No matter how stuck you feel, your efforts are not meaningless.

A LIFE BEYOND DEPRESSION

If you've been depressed for a long time, it might be hard to imagine what healing could look like. It might seem unrealistic. It might feel painful even to hope. That's okay. You don't need to create a perfect image. Just allow a few possibilities to arise.

You might wake up one morning and feel a little more at ease in your body. You might look at the sunlight shining through tree branches and feel a slight warmth in your chest. You might go for a walk and notice a gentle smile on your face. A friend might say something kind to you, and you might notice that you kind of believe it.

You begin to notice moments of joy. Not because your life is perfect, but because your heart has opened enough to let them in.

Over time, things might start to change in ways that are harder to describe. You might become someone who can feel nervous, frustrated, or sad while also experiencing self-compassion. You might find yourself giving and receiving love with more of a sense of ease.

I've worked with people who thought they'd never get better. People who had been in therapy for years, tried every medication, and were sure that nothing would work. However, when they learned to relate to themselves with kindness and compassion, things began to change. Slowly, sometimes. But the changes were real.

One woman told me she used to spend most of her day in bed, feeling like a burden to everyone around her. After 6 months of daily practice she wasn't "fixed," but she was laughing again. She had started painting. She was still tired, still human, but something inside her had come back to life.

Another client said he had always felt that he was "outside" of life, watching it happen to other people. It took almost a year for him to build enough verifying faith to engage in practice. However, just a few months later, he began to feel moments of belonging. Within another few months, his entire story about who he was and what he was capable of began to shift.

These are not miracles. They are natural results of sustained, skillful practice. This is what *viriyā* allows us to access: not a fantasy of permanent happiness, but the steady, cumulative rewards of showing up for your own life.

PRACTICE: A GLIMPSE OF WHAT'S POSSIBLE

Take a few quiet breaths. Let your attention settle.

Then ask yourself:

"If I were a little more free (or very free) from depression, what would my life feel like?"

"What would I be able to enjoy again?"

"What kind of relationships would I want to build or repair?"

"What part of me might come alive again?"

Don't force any answers. Let your mind and body respond gently, in images or phrases or emotions. If you feel nothing or if the questions are painful, that's okay. Just asking them is a kind of movement. Let whatever shows up be enough.

Then bring your hand to your chest, if that feels comfortable, and say silently:

"I want to remember why I'm practicing."

"This is for my own freedom. This is for my own life."

THE DANGER OF NOT PRACTICING

There's another side to this reflection, and it matters just as much. While we hold the beauty of what's possible, we also need to be honest about the danger of doing nothing.

Depression can convince us that nothing really matters, and that whether we practice or not, the result will be the same. But that's not true. Without practice, suffering often deepens. We grow more isolated, and our beliefs harden. Our relationships deteriorate. Our nervous system remains in a state of collapse or threat, and our life passes us by.

I want to tell you a story about my grandmother. She was a complex, fiercely intelligent person, but she lived most of her life cut off from joy. She carried deep wounds that were never tended to, and they hardened into bitterness. She had no access to the kinds of practices we're talking about in this book. She didn't trust anyone enough to let them help her.

In her later years, when I would visit her, she was still sharp, still full of opinions, but the heaviness around her was immense. Her body was stiff. Her voice often carried judgment and resentment. I never once saw her laugh. Eventually, she died holding on to her grievances, never having found a way to set them down.

With all my heart, I hope you won't live like that. Don't let your pain solidify into a permanent shape. You are not doomed to repeat the past. There are tools. There is guidance. There is another path.

SADDHĀ AND VIRIYĀ WORK TOGETHER

Saddhā and *viriyā* are distinct but connected. *Saddhā* is the confidence that change is possible, that your life can move in a different direction, and that you are capable of growth. *Viriyā* is what comes next: the willingness to put real energy into that possibility. It's the understanding that change is not only possible, but *worth the effort it takes.*

These two qualities strengthen each other. As you take small, steady steps toward healing, you begin to notice what helps. That lived experience reinforces your confidence and gives you more reason to keep going. The more you act, the more trust you build. The more trust you feel, the more energy becomes available.

If you feel a wave of resistance as you read this, that's not a reason to turn back. It may be a sign that you've touched something important. In this book, we call that an inner obstacle. If that feels true for you, jump to Section III. That part of the book will help you listen to and overcome that resistance. But if even a small part of you is ready to begin, then this might be the time. You don't need to feel fully motivated. You don't need to be entirely convinced that you'll succeed. You only need enough curiosity to try, and one small action to match it.

That is how *viriyā* begins. It doesn't need to be dramatic. It just needs to be real. One step in the direction of the life you want. One breath of effort that comes from your own clarity—not from pressure, not from shame.

Let that be enough for today. The rest will build from there.

ONE STEP AT A TIME

Before you move on, take a moment to reflect:

What's one small action I could take today that aligns with my healing?

It could be reading the next chapter. Taking three breaths with awareness. Drinking a glass of tea mindfully. Sending a kind message to someone you trust.

Then take that action. Not because it feels easy, but because *viriyā* is something we build through practice.

This is how we begin: One choice at a time. One breath. One step. One moment of energy that wasn't there before.

5

JOY IS FUEL

One of the most important teachings I ever received was this: *You don't have to fix every problem in your life before you can feel joy.*

In fact, the opposite is true. If you want to transform your suffering, you need joy. Not as a distraction, or as a reward you earn later, but as *fuel* for the work ahead.

Joy doesn't mean happiness in every moment. It doesn't mean pretending everything is fine. It comes from the willingness to notice what's not terrible in your life, even if it's small. That might mean paying attention to the taste of your favorite food, or stepping outside to look at the light shining through the leaves, or letting yourself enjoy the warmth of a cup of tea. In other words, it's giving yourself permission to enjoy something. Not later, but now. Not as a reward for getting better, but as part of how we begin.

If you feel resistant to the idea of joy or like you don't deserve it, you're not alone. That reaction is one of the most common effects of depression. Many of us have spent years postponing joy, waiting to feel more stable or worthy or productive. However, the truth is that the path of healing requires effort, and without moments of joy, we find ourselves exhausted before we've begun.

THE WORK DOESN'T NEED TO FEEL LIKE A STRUGGLE

If your efforts to change have always felt exhausting, it might be hard to imagine a different way. However, one of the most liberating things I've learned from Buddhist training is that *transformation doesn't have to feel like struggle.*

There is still effort, but that effort can feel grounded, even nourishing, when it's supported by joy.

In the previous chapter, we explored *viriyā*, the energy that drives practice. Sometimes, the reason we run out of that energy is because we're trying to push through pain without anything to sustain us. We become dry, brittle, and depleted. At that point, forcing ourselves to do more normally backfires. That's when we shift. Instead of pushing harder, we turn our attention toward cultivating joy. Even a few moments of beauty or connection can restore enough energy to take the next step.

Joy allows us to keep going. Not by denying our pain, but by reminding us that our pain isn't all there is.

THE SALT IN THE WATER

Thich Nhat Hanh used to offer a simple teaching: If you put a spoonful of salt into a glass of water, the water becomes too salty to drink.

But if you take that same spoonful of salt and throw it into a pure mountain lake, the water remains just fine.

The salt is our suffering. The water is our capacity to hold it, which is made out of the qualities of mindfulness, compassion, and joy.

When we're depleted, our inner life feels like a small glass. Even a little pain can overwhelm us. But as we cultivate joy, gratitude, and love, we expand the space around the suffering. The pain doesn't disappear, but it no longer dominates our entire experience.

This is why joy isn't a distraction or a luxury. It's what helps us hold our pain with stability and care. Without that, healing becomes impossible to sustain.

When you grow joy, you grow the container. You become someone who can be present with suffering without being consumed by it. That shift—being able to hold what hurts without collapsing—is one of the deepest fruits of practice.

Much of Section II is devoted to cultivating joy, so for now, we're just acknowledging the important role it plays in our path of transformation.

THE WISDOM OF THE BANANA LEAF

In 2005, I was living in Plum Village Monastery in France. During a question and answer program, Thich Nhat Hanh was asked about the meaning of life. In response, he told a story about meditating in the jungle during the Vietnam War. One day, he found himself sitting beside a young banana tree. It had just three leaves: one fully grown and dark green, another still curled beneath it, and a third, light and tender, just beginning to unfurl.

As he looked at the tree, something became clear. The oldest leaf was soaking in the sunshine and rain, quietly radiating beauty and peacefulness. It was fully enjoying its life as a leaf. However, that didn't mean it had abandoned the other two leaves. In nourishing itself, it was also nourishing the younger leaves, the banana tree, and in a larger sense, the whole jungle. In that moment, he saw that we are like that leaf. When we nourish ourselves with peace, love, and joy, we're not just helping ourselves. We're supporting the well-being of everyone around us.

Many of us carry the belief that caring for our own happiness is self-indulgent, especially when others are suffering. This teaching offers a very different view. When we allow ourselves to feel lightness, that lightness ripples outward.

This is the kind of joy we need on the path of healing. Not as a luxury, but as fuel and as a service. Not a private escape, but a form of deep belonging.

A PATH THAT FEEDS YOU

Section I has been about creating the conditions that make transformation possible, faith that we can change, and the energy that comes from seeing how much better life could be.

As we move forward, it's also important to find a way of practicing that nourishes you and that you can enjoy. That's what Section II is for. You'll learn how to cultivate joy, compassion, equanimity, and a wise relationship with suffering. You'll practice building the inner qualities that make healing sustainable. Not just in theory, but in the felt sense of your own life.

You don't need to feel ready. You don't need to get everything right. You'll just need the willingness to keep experimenting and seeing for yourself.

SECTION II

TRAINING YOUR MIND

6

ENJOYING THE BREATH

If you find some strong resistance to anything in this chapter, jump to Section III and see if you resonate with those practices.

Take a moment and imagine what it's like when breathing is a struggle. It could be from an asthma attack, or maybe just a really stuffy nose. You need to breathe, but it's not coming easily.

Now, come back to the present, and notice your breath in this moment. Can you breathe freely right now? Take a full breath. See what it feels like to silently say, "I'm glad I can breathe."

The breath is one of the most common tools for learning meditation. However, I believe breathing meditations are often a lot more boring than they need to be. Thich Nhat Hanh taught us that it's actually possible to learn how to *enjoy* the sensation of our breathing. If you can do that, breathing meditation doesn't feel like a chore. It can feel like a treat.

If you're depressed, your breath might feel shallow or constricted. That's okay. You don't have to force your breathing to be any specific way. Instead, you'll practice *coming home to your breath*, just as it is, and discovering that something this simple can feel like getting a massage or eating chocolate.

THE BREATH AS LIFE ENERGY

In many cultures, the word for "breath" also means the energy of life itself. In Latin, *spiritus* means both breath and spirit. In Sanskrit, *prana* means both breath and vital energy. When the Buddha taught his students to pay attention to their breathing, the word he used was like this. It meant that they should practice being aware of the air in their lungs, but also of the *energy of life itself* moving through their body.

When you breathe mindfully, you're not just calming your body or focusing your mind. You're also waking up to the fact that you are alive. Not in theory, but in this very moment. And that recognition—even if it lasts only a few seconds—can feel good.

One of the reasons we start with the breath is because it's always here. It's somewhat unique because it's something you can control, but it also happens on its own. You don't need special equipment. You don't need ideal conditions. You just need a moment of awareness and the willingness to let that moment be enough.

COMING HOME TO THE BREATH

Most of us spend our days lost in thoughts about the future or the past. However, the breath can't be found in either of those places. It's always here, in this exact moment. By turning your attention to it, you return to a place that's real, steady, and close.

PRACTICE: BASIC BREATH AWARENESS

Find a comfortable position sitting, lying down, or even standing. Close your eyes if you want, or let your gaze rest gently.

Begin by noticing the physical sensation of your breath. Where do you feel it most clearly: your nose, your chest, your belly? Let your awareness settle there.

Experiment and see how it feels to say:

"Breathing in, this feels good."

"Breathing out, this feels good."

After a couple of breaths, you can just say "in" and "out." You can also change the words to whatever feels helpful to you. Stay with this for a few minutes. If your attention wanders, just begin again. Don't try too hard or force anything.

As the breath becomes more vivid, see if you can enjoy the sensation. The coolness of the air. The rise and fall of the body. Let it be enough. Let your attention stay with your breath because it feels good, not for any other reason.

You may notice a shift in your body: a slight easing, or a feeling of steadiness. Sometimes nothing may change. Either way, the practice is to *stay with the breath* and let your awareness settle into it like coming home after a long day. If a lot of suffering arises during your practice, you can skip to Chapter 20, "Holding Suffering With Compassion."

THE BREATH CAN FEEL GOOD

For many people with depression, "enjoyment" can feel inaccessible. You don't need to force it, but you can *notice what is not wrong*. A breath that feels smooth. A moment of stillness. A little more space around your heart.

Thich Nhat Hanh taught that smiling can change our experience of the breath. Even a soft, half-smile tells the body that it's safe. It's a gesture of friendliness toward yourself. When you pair that with breath awareness, something might shift. Not all at once, but enough to begin building a relationship with the breath as a place of ease.

You might also try silently saying:

"Breathing in, I feel that I'm alive."

"Breathing out, I feel the energy of life moving through me."

If those words don't feel right, try your own. The point is to gently encourage the body and mind to reconnect, and to let the breath become a *source of nourishment*.

SAVORING THE BREATH IN DAILY LIFE

You don't have to be seated or on a cushion to enjoy your breath.

Try noticing it when you wake up, before you check your phone or get out of bed.

Notice it while washing your hands, waiting at a stoplight, or standing in line. Use small, ordinary pauses in your day to come back to your breath, even for the space of one inhale and exhale.

Each of those moments is a chance to reconnect with the energy of life inside you.

These aren't small things. They're the building blocks of presence, which has the potential to make life worth living.

THE BREATH AS A FRIEND

As you begin to work with challenging emotions, the breath can become your anchor, keeping you safe and stable in the storm. In one way, it's like a tool you "use," but it's also a relationship you cultivate.

This practice will not solve your problems, but it can *carry you through them.* Life will always have problems, and freedom comes from being able to face them with lightness and self-compassion. Your breath can be a core part of what connects you to those qualities. It can remind you that you are alive, that you are still here, that there is something in you that is still moving, and still capable of returning to this moment.

7

AWARENESS OF THE BODY

If you find some strong resistance to anything in this chapter, jump to Section III and see if you resonate with those practices.

In the *Satipaṭṭhāna Sutta*, the Buddha's foundational teaching on mindfulness, the first domain of practice is the body. That's not accidental. Thich Nhat Hanh often reminded us that coming home to the body is how we come home to the present moment. When we lose touch with our body, we lose touch with reality. But when we return to it, we return to life.

In the best possible future—one in which you've fully overcome your depression—you will experience a lot more peace, contentment, and love. However, life will also continue to include grief, disappointment, and fear.

In a good moment, many people become anxious about the good feeling ending. Instead of being able to enjoy it, they accidentally chase it away. In a painful moment, most people react in ways that make the problem worse. They might have catastrophic thoughts, desperately try to control something that is outside of their control, or just run away from their feelings altogether.

The ability to appreciate the good moments while allowing them to be temporary, and to be kind to yourself in painful moments without making them worse, is what makes emotional balance possible. This capacity is not something we're born with. It is something we train, and the training begins with mindfulness of the body.

Our thoughts aren't always true, and we can get lost in our stories. But the body speaks in sensations. It doesn't analyze or argue. It simply reveals our physiological reality in the moment. Mindfulness of the body is the most grounded way to practice nonresistance to our experience, whether it's pleasant, unpleasant, or neutral. We learn to feel our experience as it is, without needing it to be different.

As soon as you're able to feel a pleasant sensation in your body without trying to grasp it, and an unpleasant sensation without trying to run away from it, you'll find that you can respond to your life with so much more freedom.

THE PRACTICE OF SIMPLY FEELING

Many of us spend years trying to get away from what we feel in our body. We brace against tightness. We ignore discomfort. We rush to fix, adjust, or distract. Therefore, when we begin the practice of mindfulness of the body, our first task is to reverse that habit—not by trying to control or avoid the sensations, but by learning how to let them be.

This kind of practice begins with tolerance. You notice a sensation. It could be heaviness, tension, shakiness, or numbness, and you decide *I can let this be here for now*. You're not trying to enjoy it. You're just staying. It might sound like "This feels bad, but I can tolerate it."

After a little while, tolerance gives way to acceptance. You stop needing it to change. You might think, "This is okay. I don't have to fight this. I'm allowed to feel whatever I feel."

Finally, acceptance can deepen into compassion. You begin to sense the pain not just as something unpleasant, but as something tender. Something that could be held with kindness. At that point, you're not just allowing the sensation. You're taking care of it.

You don't need to force this progression. Some days you may feel only a moment of tolerance, and that's enough. The practice is to keep returning. To feel what you're feeling, as it is, without needing it to be different.

Let the body be what it is. Let the sensations come and go. With patience, your presence becomes stronger than the discomfort. That's when change becomes possible.

WHAT IT MEANS NOT TO CHANGE ANYTHING

This is subtle but important. Mindfulness of the body is not about trying to relax or fix how you feel. It's about letting go of the need to change what you're feeling.

You might notice heat, tension, hollowness, or pressure. Can you just let those sensations be there? Can you allow your body to experience what it is already experiencing without making any of it go away? If the answer is yes, even for a few seconds, something shifts. You're no longer in resistance. You're no longer fighting your own body. That nonresistance is what gives rise to healing.

Even if sensations feel intense—tightness in the chest, shakiness in the limbs—just staying with them gently, without trying to push them away, allows the body to process and release them. Over time, they may relax. But even if they don't, your relationship to them changes.

THE MAP: FROM TOLERANCE TO EMBRACE

Let's make this very practical. When you sit or lie down and scan your body, you might notice:

- Tightness in your throat.
- Heaviness in your belly.
- Numbness in your arms or legs.
- Heat or restlessness in your face.

You don't need to interpret any of it. Just feel it.

Here's the progression you're aiming for:

- *Tolerate:* "This is unpleasant, but I can tolerate it."
- *Accept:* "This is okay. I don't need to fix it."
- *Compassion:* "I see you. I'm here for you."

You don't force any stage. You just notice where you are today and offer yourself permission to be there.

A GUIDED PRACTICE: LETTING THE BODY BE

Find a comfortable posture. Close your eyes, if that feels safe.

Begin by noticing where your body touches the ground or chair.

Slowly scan through your body. Pay attention to your face, jaw, throat, chest, belly, legs.

Wherever you feel something, whether pleasant, unpleasant, or neutral, say silently, "Just feel it."

If a sensation grows stronger, stay with it. Let it grow.

If you notice thoughts like "This is too much" or "I don't like this," allow those too. Gently repeat: "It's okay to feel this. I'm here."

Stay for as long as you like. When you're ready, return to the room with a soft breath.

THE MEDICINE OF DIRECT CONTACT

Why does this work? Depression often makes the world feel distant, including our own body. That withdrawal can be a form of protection, an unconscious retreat from pain, but it comes at a cost. We stop feeling alive.

Practicing mindfulness of the body, especially without trying to change anything, is how we slowly reenter our lives. It's how we build trust with our own experience again.

As one practitioner said, "When I gave myself permission to feel this tightness, it began to relax. Not because I made it relax, but because I stopped fighting it."

IF IT FEELS TOO INTENSE

Sometimes, body awareness feels like too much. That's okay. If you start to feel flooded or overwhelmed:

- Shift to a safe part of your body: your feet, your hands, your breath.
- Open your eyes and orient to the room around you.
- Whisper to yourself, "I'm safe now. This is just a sensation."
- Or take a break. Go for a walk. Have tea. Come back later.

There is no failure here. Mindfulness is slow and kind.

8

COMING HOME TO THE PRESENT MOMENT

If you find some strong resistance to anything in this chapter, jump to Section III and see if you resonate with those practices.

Most of us don't live in the real world.

We live in remembered arguments, imagined futures, and the anticipation of what we must do next. We live in stories of our own creation, and things we wish we had done differently. Meanwhile, our body is quietly breathing. The floor is still holding us up. Life is still moving through us, breath by breath.

Coming home to the real world, just as it is, gives us a refuge from all of our imagined suffering.

NOTHING TO FIX

The practice of coming home is not about solving anything. It's about letting go of the idea that anything outside of ourselves needs to be solved before life can be okay. If we can stop chasing after the next milestone, we begin to see that *nothing is missing* in this moment. Right now, there are problems and there is beauty. Every moment of life contains both.

We might still be hurting and still be confused. But there's nothing fundamentally wrong with what's happening right now. We can sit with it. We can breathe with it. We can begin to feel human again.

That's what the Buddha called *aimlessness*. It doesn't mean giving up on healing. It means you stop believing that life will only feel worth living in some distant future when we have everything we want.

A SAFE PLACE INSIDE TIME

When you've experienced a lot of emotional pain, your nervous system may not know how to tell the difference between past danger and present safety. It might be bracing for impact all the time.

That's why we learn to ask, "Am I safe right now?"

Not in theory, but right now. This moment. Can you feel your body supported by the ground? Is there anyone threatening you? Are you in danger right now?

If not, see if you can let that truth in. Say to yourself, "In this moment, I am safe."

It's true you haven't always been safe in the past, and you won't always be safe in the future. That's true for every human being who's ever lived. However, if we can recognize the safety in this moment right now, your body has space to settle. If we ever hope to have a moment of peace, we must learn how to feel safe when we are safe.

That's the first step toward teaching your nervous system how to rest.

PRACTICE: THREE-BREATH ARRIVAL

This is one of the simplest ways to come home:

1. Take a slow inhale, and feel the breath enter your body.
2. Let yourself exhale fully, with no rush.
3. On the next breath, quietly say, “Safe here.”
4. On the next, “Safe now.”
5. Repeat one more time.

This practice is about recognizing the peace that’s already available. You don’t need to fix anything. You just need to return to this breath, this body, and this moment.

COMING HOME TO A MESS

Coming home to yourself isn’t always peaceful.

Sometimes it feels like opening the door to your bedroom and finding everything torn apart. There’s tension in your chest, shame in your gut, anger crackling through your jaw. Thoughts are loud, frantic, and mean. You walk in the door, and it’s just a mess.

Thich Nhat Hanh told a story once about a storm passing through his hermitage in France. It had been a warm afternoon, so he’d left the windows open when he went for a walk. But while he was out, the weather turned. By the time he got back, ink and paper were scattered across the room, soaked through, the wind still howling through the open windows. He didn't start cleaning right away. He didn't panic or blame himself. First, he just closed the windows.

That's the practice.

When you come home to your body and it's a mess, you don't need to fix anything right away. You just stop letting more storm in.

I had a friend in college who never cleaned his dorm room. He let food pile up, didn't do laundry, didn't take out the trash. After a while, it got so bad that he couldn't stand being in there. Eventually, he started sleeping on the couch in the common room instead.

That's how a lot of us relate to our own body and mind. Things get messy. We have too much stress, too many regrets, too many days of not checking in, and we don't want to go back in there. We keep ourselves busy, distract ourselves, do anything but come home to the wreckage.

But if we never go in, we never clean up. We just stay disconnected, floating somewhere outside of ourselves.

Coming home when your body feels like chaos starts with closing the windows. Sit down. Breathe. Don't rush to clean up the mess. Just acknowledge it. *This is what it feels like to be me right now.*

Tension in your chest? You don't need to get rid of it. Just notice it. Tightness in your stomach? Maybe put a hand there. Whisper: "I see you. I'm here." That's it.

This isn't about transcending your feelings or "reframing" them or fixing yourself. It's about the radical act of presence. Of sitting with the part of you that's in pain, without trying to make it stop hurting.

That's what it means to come home when the feelings in your

body are a mess. You walk into the wreckage. You sit down in the middle of it. You close the windows. You don't leave.

And over time, something starts to shift. Not because you forced it, but because presence itself is healing. The storm passes. The wind dies down. You pick up a few papers. You wash a dish.

You start living in your own body again.

LEARNING TO STAY WITH WHAT'S GOOD

The mind evolved to scan for problems. If you're hurting, your thoughts will often go toward what's wrong. That's not a flaw. It's survival. However, it also makes it hard to recognize what's okay.

In every moment, it's possible to find conditions for happiness. Nothing exceptional, but small, true things: The feeling of air on your face. The steadiness of your breath. A glimmer of light on the wall. The warmth of your hands.

We practice noticing those things not to be naive, but to be honest. Suffering is real, but so is beauty. Mindfulness means letting both be true.

Let yourself feel what is nourishing in this moment.

COMING HOME AGAIN AND AGAIN

At some point, you'll forget this practice. You'll get lost in thought, but that's not a failure. That's the invitation.

Each time you remember and come back, you're strengthening the part of you that knows how to return.

Right now, wherever you are, you can take one breath and say:

"This is it."

"I'm here."

"This is what's real."

Let the moment be exactly what it is. Let it be enough. Let yourself be home.

9

SHAMATHA: THE PRACTICE OF STOPPING

If you find some strong resistance to anything in this chapter, jump to Section III and see if you resonate with those practices.

There's a particular kind of stopping and resting that can bring peace and clarity.

It's not the stopping that comes from collapse or giving up. It's the kind of stopping that happens when you put something down and realize it was heavier than you thought. A kind of stillness that feels like exhaling after years of holding your breath.

In Buddhist practice, that's called *shamatha*. Sometimes it's translated as "calm abiding." But I prefer to think of it as "nowhere to go; nothing to do." We take a break from chasing any goal, from trying to achieve anything, and simply allow our body and mind to settle. We stop spinning and return to a sense of ease.

It's not a technique you apply to fix something. It's a shift in how you relate to yourself.

NOT PUSHING, NOT COLLAPSING

Depression can look like stopping from the outside. People often assume that if we're stuck in bed or can't make decisions, we must be resting. However, anyone who's been there knows that's not true. It's not resting—it's being shutdown. It's collapse. The body might be still, but the mind is racing, or fogged, or numb.

Shamatha is the opposite of that. It's not spacing out. It's not pretending to be okay. It's a deliberate, grounded kind of stillness. You're awake, but you're not bracing. You're softening, but not disappearing. You're giving yourself permission just to be, without striving, defending, or holding it all together.

In the same way that a rushing river is opaque but becomes clear when it joins a still lake, *shamatha* supports clarity in our heart and mind.

CALMING THE WHOLE BODY

The first phase of *shamatha* is letting the body begin to settle.

You don't need to do this perfectly. You don't even need to feel calm. The practice is just to stop running, internally and externally, and let your breath come to you. As you do, the nervous system starts to shift out of emergency mode.

Try the following practice.

PRACTICE: BREATHING WITH CALM

Sit, stand, or lie down.

Let your body rest.

Say silently:

"Breathing in, I allow my body to calm."

"Breathing out, I allow my body to calm."

Stay for a few breaths. Don't try to feel calm. Just let the breath move naturally, and let those words remind you that nothing is being asked of you right now.

This is not passive. It's skillful. By choosing not to chase or control, you are changing how you live in your body.

CREATING CONDITIONS, NOT OUTCOMES

Shamatha isn't about forcing peace to happen. It's about creating the conditions where peace can arise.

You can't force yourself into stillness, just like you can't force a lake to become calm. But if you stop throwing rocks in, the water will eventually settle on its own.

In the same way, if you stop feeding agitation, stop planning, regretting, judging, and comparing, something begins to shift inside you. Not immediately. Gradually, over time, your system starts to trust that it does not need to be on high alert. In that trust, calmness grows.

THIS ISN'T GIVING UP

Sometimes people think that stopping means surrendering to depression. They're afraid that if they stop pushing, they'll sink deeper. However, *shamatha* is not withdrawal. It's radical openness.

It's the practice of being fully present with yourself, without pressure. It's how we learn to rest in the middle of suffering. Not by pretending it's gone, but by allowing it to be held inside a larger space of awareness.

This space doesn't erase pain, but it softens the edges. It gives you room to breathe, and sometimes that's enough to begin again.

LETTING THE BREATH LEAD

One of the most reliable ways to practice *shamatha* is through the breath.

The breath doesn't ask anything of you. It's already happening. You don't have to control it or deepen it. Just notice it. Let your breath guide your attention inward.

You might say:

"Breathing in, I follow my breath."

"Breathing out, I allow things to be the way they are."

Each breath is a small release. Each exhale makes more space. And over time, those small movements accumulate into rest.

NOT FIXING ANYTHING

The most radical part of this practice is that there is nothing to fix.

You don't need to improve yourself. You don't need to wait until your depression lifts. You don't need to know what's next. You just need to be willing to sit down, let go of effort, and allow life to meet you as you are.

When we stop needing the moment to be different, the moment becomes bearable. Sometimes even beautiful.

PRACTICE: RESTING AS YOU ARE

Let your body find a position that feels supported.

Close your eyes if that feels safe, or keep a soft gaze.

Feel your breath moving through you.

Say silently, "This breath is enough."

Don't try to change your thoughts. Let them rise and fall.

Don't try to fix your body. Let it rest.

Just stay. Just breathe.

Just be as you are.

If you notice tension or effort creeping in, say quietly:

"Tension can come and go."

"It's all right."

Do this for a minute, or 10. You'll know when it's time to stop.

A SOFT LANDING

Effort is an important part of practice, but it's not the only important part. *Shamatha* is where we learn the other side: *how to rest.* How to stop carrying so much. How to let the ground hold us.

It's a soft landing.

If you practice coming back to that place of calm, even just for a few breaths at a time, it begins to change you. Not dramatically. Not all at once. But steadily. Quietly. Like water shaping stone.

Let this practice be a place where you don't have to try.

Let it be where you learn to be held.

10

INFINITE CONDITIONS

If you find some strong resistance to anything in this chapter, jump to Section III and see if you resonate with those practices.

Every moment of life contains infinite conditions for suffering, and every moment contains infinite conditions for joy.

That may not feel true. Especially when you're depressed, the pain tends to fill up your field of view until it becomes the only thing you can see. However, depression doesn't mean the joyful conditions have disappeared. It means the spotlight isn't pointing at them.

Take a moment and imagine writing two lists. One for every possible thing that you *could* be upset about, and one for every possible thing that you *could* be grateful for. The first might include disappointment, exhaustion, shame, trauma, loneliness. The second might include clean drinking water, the breath in your lungs, someone who once made you laugh, the warmth of a blanket, the steadiness of the ground beneath you.

Both lists would be infinitely long.

Neither list is wrong, but when you're depressed, only one tends to dominate your attention.

TRAINING THE SPOTLIGHT

The mind is always rehearsing something. Left to itself, it rehearses what's missing, what's unresolved, and what might go wrong. That's not a personal flaw. It's part of how the brain evolved to anticipate danger, solve problems, and remember pain so we don't repeat it.

If you rehearse your suffering every day, it becomes a habit. The longer that habit goes unchallenged, the more convincing it feels. Eventually, suffering starts to feel like the whole truth.

This chapter is not about ignoring suffering. It's about recognizing that joy is also available in this moment. If we never take time to notice it, we cut ourselves off from one of the most reliable sources of strength we have.

When you remember that both lists exist, it becomes possible to gently train your attention toward balance.

YOU DON'T NEED TO FEEL GRATEFUL

This practice is about being in touch with reality, not forcing yourself to feel any specific way.

Sometimes noticing what's beautiful actually brings grief. You feel the softness of your pillow, and you realize how long it's been since you felt held. You hear a bird singing, and your heart breaks a little because you don't feel ready to sing.

That's okay.

The purpose is not to cheer yourself up. It is to stop ignoring what is beautiful in the world.

Even if your depression tells you that joy is gone, it's not gone.

It's simply out of view. The sun doesn't disappear because the curtain is closed. You can choose to open it—even a little—and let some light in.

WHAT ELSE IS TRUE?

This is one of the most useful questions I know. When your mind is absorbed in a painful thought or a spiral of discouragement, you can pause and ask:

"What else is true right now?"

"What's not wrong in this moment?"

You might be feeling a loss, but what hasn't been lost? You might feel pain, but where can you find beauty?

Nothing needs to be inspiring or profound. You are not mining for inspiration. You are allowing the moment to be more complete.

When you ask what else is true, you're not arguing with pain. You're just refusing to let it be the only voice in the room.

WHAT YOU WATER GROWS

The Buddha taught that the mind is like a garden. Every day, seeds are watered. Some are seeds of fear, resentment, despair. Others are seeds of calm, connection, contentment. Every moment of attention is a drop of water.

When we focus only on what's wrong, we strengthen the seeds of suffering. When we take time to notice what's good, even briefly, we water something different.

This doesn't mean forcing yourself to feel better. It means building the capacity to stay balanced. If you can let your attention rest on one small, good thing each day, you begin to change the texture of your inner life.

You don't need joy to be big. You just need to remember where to look.

YOU ARE NOT A CLOSED SYSTEM

Nothing you feel arises from nowhere. Every emotion, every pattern, every painful belief is the result of causes and conditions. And causes and conditions always change.

You are not a closed system.

Whatever has been dominant in your life—grief, fear, or disappointment—those aren't personal failures. They are the outcomes of a set of conditions. When you shift the conditions, even slightly, you begin to shift the outcome.

That's what this practice is. Not an argument with what is, but a quiet act of tending what could be.

You start by recognizing that joy, too, has causes. Joy is not the reward for healing. It is a source of energy for healing. And you already have access to more than enough conditions for joy if you can find a way to notice them.

11

FROGLESSNESS

If you find some strong resistance to anything in this chapter, jump to Section III and see if you resonate with those practices.

During the years I spent training with my teacher, Thich Nhat Hanh, one of the most striking phrases he would use was "the attainment of froglessness." He said it with a smile, but it wasn't a joke. He described it as one of the first true fruits of practice that people begin to notice when they start meditation training.

He asked us to picture a frog placed in the center of a plate. The frog, of course, doesn't stay still. It jumps. Place it back in the center, and it jumps again. Always leaping toward something else.

The mind is like that. Even when the body is still, the mind rarely stays in one place. It's already off to the next problem, the next memory, the next imagined conversation, or the next imagined version of yourself. However, through training, we can teach the mind to rest, which allows it to heal.

Froglessness is that capacity.

THE FIRST FRUIT OF PRACTICE

Thich Nhat Hanh described froglessness as the *first attainment* in meditation. Not enlightenment. Not insight. Just the ability to stay with what is actually happening.

If you can stay with what is present in the real world and in yourself for the space of a breath, you've attained a bit of froglessness. You don't need to be still for an hour. Just still for a moment. One breath where your mind doesn't jump.

WHAT FROGLESSNESS IS NOT

People sometimes assume that depression is a kind of stillness. From the outside, it can look that way: like the person has stopped moving, stopped trying, stopped caring. However, research on attention shows that the depressed mind is often *more* restless than usual. It jumps constantly. Not outward, but inward—looping through fears, regrets, comparisons, self-judgment. A depressed mind is not a settled mind. It's a mind stuck in a small enclosure, pacing in circles.

Froglessness is something else entirely. It's a form of presence. A quiet, alert willingness to stay in contact with the moment, whether that moment is pleasant, unpleasant, or neutral.

TRAINING THE MIND TO STAY

The mind will jump. That's not failure. That's just a normal mind. Each time you notice it, you have a chance to come back. You're not trying to make the frog behave. You're teaching it, slowly, that it's safe to rest.

The most skillful way to begin this training is through the body. The breath is helpful. So are the soles of your feet, the sensation of your hands resting, the feeling of the spine held upright. These are places that don't leap. They're already here.

If you can enjoy being in touch with one of those anchors, then the mind won't want to jump. Stay for a moment. Then another. If your mind jumps, that's okay. Gently place it back.

This is not about suppressing thought. It's about changing your relationship to movement. You're not following every leap. You're not chasing yourself. You're learning how to be still without needing the world, or yourself, to be different.

PRACTICE: ONE MINUTE OF FROGLESSNESS

Try this:

- Sit comfortably.
- Let your hands rest in your lap or on your knees.
- Feel your body in contact with the ground.
- Take one slow breath.
- Say silently: "I can enjoy being right here. I don't need to jump."

- Rest your attention in the body—not to analyze, just to feel.
- Stay for 1 minute. If the mind moves, guide it back. Not with force. Just gently, like placing a child back in bed.

That's the whole practice.

You don't need to feel peaceful. You don't need to achieve anything. The fruit of this practice is simply this: You stayed.

STILLNESS THAT HEALS

There is a kind of healing that only happens when we stop trying to improve the moment.

Froglessness allows the nervous system to downshift. It creates space for the body to soften and the mind to let go. It teaches you that you don't always need to respond, or explain, or escape. That you can be in contact with life as it is, and not be overwhelmed by it.

Over time, this stillness becomes a refuge. Not because you're shutting out the world, but because you've stopped abandoning yourself.

When the frog rests, you begin to remember that it's possible to rest too.

12

CULTIVATING JOY

If you find some strong resistance to anything in this chapter, jump to Section III and see if you resonate with those practices.

In Buddhism, joy and happiness are related but not the same. Joy comes first. It has a spark of energy, freshness, and even a little excitement. Happiness comes later. It is quieter. It carries the flavor of contentment and ease. Both are important, and both can be cultivated.

Thich Nhat Hanh would sometimes say, "A good practitioner knows how to manifest a feeling of joy." He didn't mean faking it. He meant that joy can be generated intentionally, the way a gardener knows how to water seeds. With practice, joy becomes more available, even in difficult times.

THE SOURCES OF JOY

There are many ways joy can arise. Four in particular are emphasized in Buddhist practice: letting go, mindfulness, concentration, and understanding.

Letting Go

One of the deepest sources of joy is release. So much of our suffering comes from the belief that we cannot be happy until conditions change: until we get what we want or until our pain is gone. Joy becomes possible the moment we let go of that belief. When we allow ourselves to stop postponing happiness, even for a breath, the mind feels lighter. Letting go is not resignation. It is freedom from the story that life has to be different before we are allowed to feel joy.

Mindfulness

Another source of joy is simply noticing the positive conditions already present in our lives. That noticing is the essence of mindfulness. The air entering our lungs. The presence of someone who has been kind to us. The stability of the ground under our feet. When we pay attention, we see that life always contains more than our pain. We don't have to pretend the suffering isn't there. We simply open to a fuller picture. That wider frame makes space for something nourishing.

Concentration

Joy also grows when the mind gathers itself. Normally our attention is scattered, pulled in many directions at once. We think about the past, anticipate the future, and spin stories in the present. This fragmentation creates fatigue. When we practice mindfulness, our attention begins to collect. The mind becomes concentrated instead of divided. That concentration is itself a source of joy, like light made stronger when it passes through a lens.

Understanding

Understanding is the fourth cause of joy. As the mind becomes more collected, we begin to see ourselves and the world with greater clarity. We recognize that our suffering has causes and conditions, and that it can change. We see that other people, like us, are trying to find their way. We start to understand, not just intellectually, but with our whole being. With that understanding comes something surprising: love.

When we understand anyone or anything deeply enough, even ourselves, we can't help but love them. Understanding reveals the story behind the struggle, the causes behind the behavior. It lets us see not just what someone did, but why. When we understand deeply enough, we see a living being that is suffering and wants love. In that moment, our heart opens. That's what makes this kind of understanding a source of joy. It doesn't erase difficulty, but it turns judgment into compassion and isolation into connection. It fills the space around our pain with love.

PRACTICING JOY

Cultivating joy is not about denying pain. It is about creating balance. If suffering is always available, and joy is always available, we need the capacity to notice both. We need to practice touching the seeds of joy so that they grow stronger.

You might experiment with this reflection: *What conditions for joy are already here?*

The question itself is an act of mindfulness. It doesn't require a certain answer. Sometimes it points to something obvious. Other times it reveals something small but steady: the trees outside your window, a breath that feels grounding, a moment of silence.

Each time you recognize a condition for joy, you water that seed. Over time, those seeds begin to sprout more often. Joy is no longer a rare visitor. It becomes part of the landscape of your life.

JOY AS MEDICINE

Depression tells us that joy is out of reach. Buddhist practice says otherwise. Joy is not a distant reward. It is a source of energy for the path itself. When you learn how to cultivate joy through letting go, mindfulness, concentration, and understanding, you discover that joy supports healing, just as healing supports joy.

Joy may start small. That's enough. Every drop of joy is a drop of medicine. It reminds you that even in the midst of difficulty, your life still contains beauty, and your heart still contains the capacity to feel it.

13

CULTIVATING HAPPINESS

If you find some strong resistance to anything in this chapter, jump to Section III and see if you resonate with those practices.

In Pali, the language of the original Buddhist sutras, the word for suffering is *dukkha*, and the word for happiness is *sukha*. These are both words that refer to the wheels of a carriage. If the axle hole in your wheel is bad and you're constantly getting jostled around, the word is *dukkha*. If the axle hole in your wheel is good, that is *sukha*, a smooth ride.

Sukha is normally translated as "happiness," but sometimes it's closer to the word "ease." It is not what happens when you get what you want. It's more like the contentment that arises from being at peace with the way things are.

In the *Discourse on Mindfulness of Breathing* (*Anapanasati Sutta*), the Buddha describes a natural sequence. First, we breathe and become aware of the body. Then we cultivate joy—which is more energetic, and has the flavor of delight. Then, when the body and mind are no longer restless, something deeper appears: *sukha*, contented happiness and ease.

This chapter is about learning how to notice that kind of happiness, and how to stay with it long enough to let it grow.

A DIFFERENT KIND OF HAPPINESS

In the modern world, we're surrounded by promises of happiness. Buy this. Achieve that. Become someone new. The happiness being sold to us is often a kind of excitement, dressed up as satisfaction.

In Buddhist practice, happiness has a different flavor. It is not something we chase. It is something we allow.

You don't create happiness by forcing yourself to feel better. You create the conditions for it by calming your breath, settling your body, and letting your mind rest in the moment as it is. Then happiness arises on its own.

THE BREATH THAT LEADS YOU HOME

One of the simplest ways to touch happiness is to come back to the breath:

> "Breathing in, I allow ease to arise if it wants to."
>
> "Breathing out, I allow happiness to arise if it wants to."

Sometimes, we might discover that happiness is already here. We just didn't notice it.

HAPPINESS LIVES IN SIMPLICITY

You don't need a breakthrough. You don't need to be completely healed. Happiness often begins with small things:

- The sound of birds in the morning.
- A warm cup of tea held with both hands.
- A quiet moment of true rest.

These experiences are not superficial. They are part of what makes life livable. When you allow yourself to fully receive them, they become medicine.

If you can let the moment be enough, even for a breath, you've already touched happiness.

LETTING GO OF THE IDEA OF HAPPINESS

One of the most common obstacles to happiness is the belief that it has to look a certain way.

We think we'll be happy when the pain is gone, when we've found clarity, when we've finally arrived at some imagined version of ourselves. However, that image is an illusion. It keeps moving. And while we chase it, we miss the reality of the moment: this breath, this body, this life.

Thich Nhat Hanh used to say, "If you know what happiness looks like, you'll never be happy." He wasn't discouraging us from cultivating joy. He was reminding us that clinging to a fixed idea of happiness keeps us from the real thing.

Let that idea go. Allow for the possibility that happiness is already available, right now.

PRACTICE: NOTICING EASE

Try this:

- Sit comfortably and feel your breath entering and leaving your body.
- Without needing to change anything, ask, "Is there any part of me that feels okay right now?"
- Maybe it's your hands resting in your lap. Maybe it's the rhythm of your breath. Maybe it's a small sense of relief that you're doing nothing at all.
- If a thought arises that you need your circumstances to change before happiness could be possible, see if you can let go of whatever imagined thing you believe you need.
- Rest your attention there for a few breaths. Let the energy of ease expand if it wants to.

You don't have to force happiness. You allow it to arise when it's ready.

WHY THIS MATTERS

When you're depressed, happiness may feel irrelevant. Even threatening. There's a part of the mind that believes it must stay vigilant—must keep suffering in view at all times or something important will be missed.

Yet suffering doesn't need your full attention. It's already had enough. You can let yourself rest. Even if just for a minute.

This isn't pretending. It's remembering that happiness and sorrow often live side by side. You're allowed to feel both.

If you give happiness a little space, it can begin to grow.

14

DEEP RELAXATION

If you find some strong resistance to anything in this chapter, jump to Section III and see if you resonate with those practices.

There is a kind of exhaustion that goes deeper than sleep can touch. The kind that builds up from months or years of trying to hold yourself together, pushing through sadness, shame, anxiety, and pretending to be okay because the world doesn't always make space for anything else. When you live like that long enough, your body forgets what real rest feels like.

Depression doesn't always mean collapse. Often it means functioning through fog, smiling when you don't feel anything, making it through the day and then lying awake at night, as your body feels wired and heavy at the same time. When your nervous system has forgotten how to let go, when your muscles never quite unclench, and your chest doesn't rise all the way on the in-breath. That's when we need deep relaxation. Not as a luxury, but as medicine.

REST AS MEDICINE

In the Plum Village tradition, deep relaxation is a formal practice. It's usually done lying down, eyes closed, with a gentle voice guiding. You start at the crown of the head and move slowly downward, as your awareness traces each body part—eyes, jaw, shoulders, hands, belly, legs—inviting it to rest if it's ready to. You don't force anything. You don't try to feel better. You just let your awareness touch what's there, without demand.

Thich Nhat Hanh often reminded us that healing begins with rest. Not just the absence of activity, but the presence of peace. He said that after a forest burns, it doesn't grow back the next day. It needs time—stillness, water, protection from further harm. Your body is no different. If you're suffering from depression, you may already know this instinctively. You're tired all the time, and yet sleep doesn't help. That's because the kind of rest you need isn't just physical. It's the kind of rest that tells your body: *You don't have to brace anymore. You are safe here.*

YOU DON'T HAVE TO FEEL BETTER FIRST

One of the reasons this practice can be so helpful for depression is that it doesn't require that you feel better. You don't have to be motivated, inspired, or even hopeful. You just have to lie down and listen. You meet your body exactly as it is. You let go of the need to fix anything. And in that letting go, something begins to shift. Not because you made it shift, but because the conditions for healing are finally present.

This is an act of rebellion against the productivity culture that tells us we have to earn our rest. It's a refusal to participate in the belief that you only get to stop when everything else is done. It's a way of saying, "This body is worthy of care now, exactly as it is."

LETTING GO OF EFFORT

As you practice deep relaxation, you may notice pockets of tension that never went away—not because you weren't trying hard enough, but because trying was part of the problem. The effort to hold everything together becomes its own kind of stress. Deep relaxation invites you to let the holding go. Not all at once. Just a little. Just enough to remember that rest is possible.

Sometimes the mind will resist. It may say, "You should be doing something" or "This isn't helping." That's okay. The mind has been trained to expect urgency. You don't need to argue with it. Just come back to the breath. Come back to your shoulders. Come back to the feeling of the ground underneath you.

YOU CAN'T FAIL AT THIS

If you fall asleep during the practice, that's fine. If you don't feel anything profound, that's fine too. What matters is that you're creating the conditions for ease. You're planting a seed. And even if you don't feel it right away, the body remembers. Each time you return to deep relaxation, you're sending the message: *I'm not abandoning you. You don't have to be tense to survive.*

In Buddhism, the body is not separate from the mind. When the body is held in tension, the mind has no ground to rest on. When the body is invited to release, the mind can soften too. This is not about bliss or transcendence. This is about learning to come home.

Sometimes when you let go of the chronic tension, surprising emotions can arise. You might encounter some grief that has been locked away for a long time. Sometimes the simple act of breathing, letting go, and resting your attention on your own belly is the first opportunity your grief has found to receive your attention. Don't run away from it. It has been exiled for a long time, and needs some love..

Deep relaxation is not a cure, but it is a foundation. It's a way of creating the space in which healing becomes possible, just because you allowed it. In a culture that worships effort, this practice teaches trust.

Sometimes, you don't need to do more. You need to rest.

GUIDED PRACTICE: DEEP RELAXATION

This practice can be done lying down in a quiet space, using a recording or your own internal voice. You can also search the internet for videos of "Plum Village deep relaxation," which will provide you the voice of a monastic to guide you. If possible, give yourself 20–30 minutes without interruptions.

1. Find your resting posture.

   Lie on your back, arms gently resting by your sides or on your belly.
   Let your feet fall naturally outward.
   Close your eyes if that feels safe.
   Feel the ground supporting you.

2. Breathing in, I arrive. Breathing out, I let go.

    Follow the natural rhythm of your breath.

    With each exhale, allow gravity to do just a little more of the work.

    Let the body settle. Imagine that you're giving your body to the earth.

3. Bring attention to the crown of your head.

    Breathing in, I am aware of the top of my head.

    Breathing out, I let it be soft.

4. Move down through your face.

    Eyes. Cheeks. Jaw. Is there any clenching?

    Breathing in, I notice my jaw. Breathing out, I release it.

    Thank you, jaw, for helping me speak and eat. Now you can rest.

5. Neck and shoulders.

    These are often the most burdened parts of us.

    Breathing in, I feel my shoulders. Breathing out, I let them rest.

    Thank you, neck and shoulders, for holding me up all day. Now you can rest.

6. Arms and hands.

    Bring awareness through each arm, elbow, wrist, palm, fingers.

    You don't need to feel anything special. Just notice.

7. Chest and heart.

    Breathing in, I feel my chest rise. Breathing out, I soften around my heart.

    If there is emotion here, let it be. You're just saying, "I'm here."

    Thank you to my heart, which keeps me alive. You can relax.

8. Belly and abdomen.

    Let the breath be gentle and low.

    Breathing in, I feel my belly rise. Breathing out, I let it go.

    This is often where tension hides. You don't need to push it away. Just stay.

9. Pelvis and hips.

    The seat of much emotion and memory.

    Let this region sink toward the earth.

    Breathing in, I feel the heaviness of the hips. Breathing out, I allow rest.

10. Legs, knees, ankles, and feet.

    Slowly scan through the legs, letting the attention move downward.

    Feel your feet resting on the earth.

    Imagine the tension flowing out through the soles.

    Thank you to my legs and feet that carry me around. You can rest.

11. Rest in the whole body.

    Let go of scanning. Let go of doing.

    Breathing in, I feel my whole body lying here. Breathing out, I allow it to rest.

Let yourself stay here as long as you like. If the mind wanders, that's okay. If emotion comes, that's okay. Let the ground hold all of it.

When you're ready to end the practice, gently wiggle your fingers and toes. Bring a hand to your heart. Take one more conscious breath.

15

MOUTH YOGA

If you find some strong resistance to anything in this chapter, jump to Section III and see if you resonate with those practices.

It's clear that your mind affects your body. You can often tell how someone is feeling by looking at their posture or their face. If you have a fearful thought or recall a beautiful memory, your facial expression and body language will change accordingly.

What's less obvious, but just as powerful, is that your body affects your mind. How you sit, how you breathe, and even the shape of your face can change how you feel.

In Buddhist practice, we learn to shift the body gently. Not as a performance, but to offer the mind a new message. When we soften our face or allow a small smile to arise, we are telling the nervous system: *Right now, there is no emergency. Right now, it's okay to rest.*

THE SMILE AS A DOORWAY

Thich Nhat Hanh called this practice *mouth yoga*. The idea is simple: Bring gentle awareness to your face, and allow a soft, natural smile to appear. Not a performative smile, not a social mask, but a real expression of presence.

Sometimes he would describe this as a "half-smile," just enough to relax the muscles in your face and invite a shift in your internal weather. You're not smiling *because* you feel happy. You're smiling to *support* happiness. Like a subtle gesture of friendliness toward your own experience.

This kind of smile is an invitation back to the present moment. It signals that you are safe enough, steady enough, and free enough to inhabit your body fully. It feels like allowing your face to relax and seeing if a smile might want to manifest.

WHAT SMILING IS (AND ISN'T)

Smiling in this tradition is not forced. It's not about suppressing grief or pretending that everything is fine.

It's a mindfulness practice. A physical expression of self-compassion. When you smile in this way, you are offering a gift to yourself. You are reminding yourself that your well-being is not entirely at the mercy of external conditions.

Thich Nhat Hanh once called it a "revolutionary act." A moment of not being ruled by fear. A way of saying, with your whole body, "I am not a victim of this moment. I can choose how to relate to it."

SMILING AND THE BREATH

One of the simplest and most effective practices is to coordinate your smile with your breath. As you inhale, say silently:

"Breathing in, I calm my body."

"Breathing out, I smile."

This practice helps unify the body and mind. The breath becomes smoother. The body begins to settle. You may not feel instantly joyful, but you might notice a drop of ease or a flicker of peace. That's enough.

Over time, this becomes a way to reset. A way to return to yourself when you feel scattered, overwhelmed, or flat.

SMILING AS A DAILY PRACTICE

There are many opportunities to weave *mouth yoga* into your day:

- *Morning poem (gāthā).* Upon waking, try silently saying:
  - "Waking up this morning, I smile.
  - Twenty-four brand new hours are before me.
  - I vow to live fully in each moment, and to look at all beings with eyes of compassion."

This is not about setting lofty goals. It's about waking up into gratitude and choice.

- *Bell practice.* Choose one daily activity (such as taking a shower or your first sip of coffee) and let it be a cue to stop, take a breath, and smile. This kind of stopping recalibrates your system.

- *Telephone meditation.* Let the phone ring once or twice before answering. Use that moment to breathe in—*calm*—and breathe out—*smile*. Then pick up the phone with presence.

SMILING WITH THE BODY

In deep relaxation practice, we sometimes smile to different parts of the body. It sounds strange at first, but it can be deeply healing. You scan through the body slowly, breathing with awareness, and offering a smile to each part:

"Breathing in, I'm aware of my eyes."

"Breathing out, I smile to my eyes."

You continue: smiling to your jaw, your shoulders, your stomach, your hands. You linger in the places that hold pain. Not to fix them, but to soften around them. Smiling is how we say, "I see you, and I'm staying with you."

This is not about self-improvement. It's about kindness. It's about reinhabiting your body after fear or numbness has pushed you out.

THE FUNCTION OF THE SMILE

The half-smile tells the body: *There's no need to struggle right now.*

That simple message does more than you might expect. It slows your heart rate. It steadies your breath. It quiets the part of the mind that's still preparing for a fight. It allows the present moment to feel more inhabitable.

When depression makes everything feel hollow or flat, *mouth yoga* is one way to gently invite some warmth back in. Not by pretending to be happy, but by loosening the grip of despair.

You may not always feel like smiling. That's okay. You don't have to force it. But when the moment feels right, try it. Just a half-smile. Just for a few breaths.

16

WATERING POSITIVE SEEDS

If you find some strong resistance to anything in this chapter, jump to Section III and see if you resonate with those practices.

Buddhist psychology teaches that every possible mental state—happiness, fear, curiosity, and hopelessness—exists as a seed (*bīja*) in the garden of our mind. In this garden, all the seeds are waiting in the soil for the right conditions to sprout.

If something waters your seed of anger, it will manifest as a feeling. Then when conditions change, it will return to its seed form in the soil. This garden is special because every time a certain seed (like anger or gratitude) sprouts, the seed itself becomes stronger. Next time, it will be easier to manifest. Eventually, if a seed is strong enough, just the tiniest amount of watering will make it show up.

Therefore, the practice is learning how to tend this field.

As the gardener, you don't control what's in the soil, but you do choose what to water. When you rehearse everything in your life that's gone wrong, you are watering the seeds of resentment and despair. When you choose to help someone in need, you are watering the seed of kindness.

You're always watering something. The question is What do you want to grow?

NOTICING WHAT YOU'RE WATERING

Most of us spend a lot of time watering the same handful of seeds: fear, regret, comparison, and anxiety. That's not because we want to suffer. It's because those are the habits we've developed over the course of our lives. When the mind feels pain, it scans for more pain. When it feels threatened, it searches for threats. These patterns become automatic.

However, with awareness, we can choose differently.

We can pause in the middle of the loop and ask, "Is there another seed I could water right now? Could I water something in me that brings steadiness?"

This is not about suppressing or denying the pain. It's about widening your view. You are not only your fear. You are also your patience, your humor, your capacity to breathe and keep going.

Those seeds need water too.

POSITIVE SEEDS MUST BE STRONG ENOUGH TO HOLD THE PAIN

Sometimes people misunderstand this teaching. They hear about watering positive seeds and assume it means ignoring what's difficult. That's not the point at all.

We water positive seeds because we need them to be strong enough to embrace our suffering. If you're going to do the work of transformation, of really facing your pain, you need something inside you that's big enough to hold it.

That something is built over time. It's built by nourishing joy, gratitude, compassion, and equanimity. Those qualities don't compete with the pain. Instead, they are the qualities we use to bring loving-awareness and healing to our suffering.

It's not about choosing love and ignoring fear. It's about choosing love so you can love your fear.

That's what we're doing here.

PRACTICE: FIVE BREATHS OF NOURISHMENT

This practice is simple. You can do it anytime:

- Sit or lie down. Let your hands rest gently.
- Take five slow breaths.
- On each inhale, say silently:

  "Breathing in, I water a seed of peace" (or any other quality you choose).
- On each exhale, say:

  "Breathing out, I let it grow."

You don't need to feel anything in particular. Your awareness is already watering something.

EVERY ACT WATERS SOMETHING

You don't have to be sitting on a meditation cushion to do this practice.

When you listen to soothing music, you're watering a seed. When you text a friend with love, eat a meal slowly, or let yourself enjoy the sky for a moment, you're watering something. The more you do this, the easier it becomes to remember that those seeds are real. You don't need to feel good to nourish them. You only need to remember they're there.

You're not starting from scratch. You've laughed before. You've cared before. You've sat through difficulty and made it through. All of that is still in you, waiting for the watering can.

YOU CAN TRUST WHAT'S GROWING

The gardener doesn't dig up the soil every day to check the roots. They plant the seeds, water them, make sure the ground is warm and protected, and then they trust.

This is part of the practice too. You don't need to measure your progress every day. You don't need to feel transformed in order for transformation to be happening.

Keep watering what matters, even when it feels small. Especially when it feels small. Let your joy, your compassion, your steadiness become big enough to hold the rest.

That's where healing begins.

17

SANGHA: JOYFULLY TOGETHER

If you find some strong resistance to anything in this chapter, jump to Section III and see if you resonate with those practices.

When you're hurting, community can feel out of reach. It might feel safer to isolate, or you might believe you have to feel okay before connecting with others. However, in Buddhism we learn that *sangha*, "spiritual community," is one of the conditions that makes healing possible.

Thich Nhat Hanh often said that "a true *sangha* is not a club or a social circle." It is a field of shared mindfulness, concentration, and insight. When we practice in community, our individual awareness is supported by the collective. Just like a small candle shines brighter when surrounded by others, your ability to be present becomes stronger in the company of a practicing community.

Even the Buddha, after his enlightenment, didn't keep teaching alone. He built a *sangha*. He knew that community was not a luxury. It was part of the path.

YOU DON'T HAVE TO BE OKAY FIRST

Many people believe they need to fix themselves before they can belong. The truth is the opposite. You don't need to be perfect to be supported by a *sangha*. The *sangha* exists precisely so you don't have to carry everything alone.

When you're overwhelmed, you can lean on the collective steadiness. Thich Nhat Hanh would compare it to being a drop of water that joins a river, or someone carrying a heavy load who steps into a boat. The *sangha* helps carry the weight so you don't sink.

You don't have to be impressive. You don't have to speak. You only need to arrive.

IF YOU'RE ALONE RIGHT NOW

If you don't have people in your life right now who feel like *sangha*, that's okay. You're starting from the same place that many people do. You are not truly alone. Your *sangha* might be waiting for you to find it.

The most important thing is to remember that *sangha* can take many forms. It could be a local meditation group that meets in your town or a Zoom meeting with people whose names you don't even know. It could be a church, a 12-step group, or a community organized around another spiritual tradition. What matters isn't the label. It's the shared aspiration. Find some people who are trying to develop the same kinds of qualities you want for yourself: compassion, patience, mindfulness, understanding. Then, be a drop of water and join their river.

If you're able to attend something in person, that can be wonderful. Physical presence, walking, sitting, or even drinking tea alongside others can be particularly good for calming the nervous system. If you're not ready for that, or it's not available, try something online. You can start by simply listening in. You don't have to speak, you don't have to turn on your camera. Just let yourself feel the presence of others practicing together.

It doesn't have to feel comfortable. You just have to be willing to experiment with the possibility that connection might be available.

THE JOY OF PRACTICING TOGETHER

When we practice with others, something subtle begins to change. The room becomes more still, our breath deepens, and our inner chaos is soothed by the presence of those around us.

This is not about losing yourself. It's about remembering that you don't have to hold everything alone.

The teachings of Thich Nhat Hanh include practical tools for keeping *sangha* life supportive and harmonious:

- *The six harmonies (six concords)*: These include sharing time, space, and understanding; practicing ethical conduct together; speaking with kindness; and making decisions by consensus.

- *Beginning anew*: A structured, gentle process of reconciliation, offering appreciation, expressing regrets, naming hurts, and proposing ways forward. The book *Beginning*

Anew by Sister Chan Khong is a great resource for this practice.

- *Dharma sharing circles*: Spaces where people listen deeply without giving advice. The agreement is simple: Speak from the heart and listen without judgment.
- *Hospitality practices*: Welcoming newcomers, acknowledging effort, and recognizing one another's goodness as a deliberate part of the path.

None of these are complicated, but they are powerful. They teach us how to live with others in ways that support, not drain, our practice. If you want to find a *sangha* that practices in this tradition, look for "Plum Village *sanghas*" online.

HOW SANGHA HELPS WITH DEPRESSION

When you're depressed, being around others can feel exhausting. However, feeling seen and supported by others who are also practicing (not judging or fixing, just practicing) can be a lifeline.

Sangha offers refuge, not performance. You're not expected to impress anyone. You only have to breathe.

The healing isn't always dramatic. It might just be the feeling of sitting next to someone who's breathing mindfully and the awareness that you're not alone. Sometimes the moment of shared silence feels like belonging.

SMALL WAYS TO BEGIN

- Take two slow breaths, then text one person: "Would you be willing to talk with me about a book I'm reading?"

That is *sangha*.

- Join an online meditation group, even once. Let the field carry you.
- Find a local meditation group and attend one meeting. See if practice feels easier in that context. If it doesn't, you don't have to go back.

JOYFULLY TOGETHER

The title of one of Thich Nhat Hanh's books is *Joyfully Together*. That phrase is more than wishful thinking. It's a deep expression of what's possible when we choose community over isolation.

When we practice together, joy becomes more accessible. We learn to share suffering and joy without needing to solve anything. The *sangha* becomes a place where your nervous system can rest, your mind can settle, and your heart can remember that it still belongs.

18

WHAT IS KARUṆĀ?: COMPASSION WITH EQUANIMITY

If you find some strong resistance to anything in this chapter, jump to Section III and see if you resonate with those practices.

In English, the word "compassion" can mean many different things. Sometimes it refers to tenderness or pity. Sometimes it carries a sense of passivity, as though compassion is simply watching someone suffer and wishing them well. Other times it is used almost sentimentally, in a way that feels sweet but not particularly strong.

In Buddhism, the word *karuṇā* has a much more precise meaning. It is not pity. It is not sentimental. *Karuṇā* is the heartfelt wish that suffering be relieved, combined with the understanding and acceptance that suffering is inevitable. Another way of saying this is that compassion, in Buddhism, always contains equanimity.

This is what makes *karuṇā* different from what we often call compassion in everyday English. *Karuṇā* doesn't collapse under pain, and it doesn't distance itself either. It is the strength to be present with suffering because it understands that suffering is part of life.

THE BRAHMAVIHĀRAS AS ONE ATTITUDE

Karuṇā is one of the four *brahmavihāras*, sometimes translated as the "divine abodes" or "limitless qualities" of the awakened heart. The four are:

- *Mettā*: loving-kindness—the wish that others be well.
- *Karuṇā*: compassion—the wish that suffering be relieved.
- *Muditā*: sympathetic joy—happiness in the happiness of others.
- *Upekkhā*: equanimity—the capacity to stay steady and open to all of it.

These are not separate qualities. They are facets of one unified attitude toward life. Together they sound something like this:

"I want you to be well." (*mettā*)

"I don't want you to suffer." (*karuṇā*)

"If you are happy, it makes me happy." (*muditā*)

"And I know and accept that you will suffer sometimes." (*upekkhā*)

Each quality balances the others. Loving-kindness without equanimity can become clinging. Compassion without equanimity becomes burnout. Equanimity without compassion drifts into indifference. Only when they are practiced together does each one mature fully.

HOLDING PAIN WITHOUT COLLAPSING

Think of how you hold a crying baby. You don't ignore them, and you don't scold them. You don't panic or try to solve everything at once. You simply hold the baby with presence and warmth, saying, "It's okay for you to cry. If there's anything I can do, I'm here."

That is *karuṇā*. It is compassion with equanimity, a way of being present with pain that accepts it fully, while also desiring its easing.

This is the kind of presence we can cultivate toward ourselves. We can learn to hold our fear, grief, or shame the way we would hold that baby. Not to get rid of it, but to stay steady and kind in its presence. From there, transformation becomes possible.

THE NEAR ENEMIES

The Buddhist tradition warns of "near enemies," which are qualities that look similar to the *brahmavihāras* but distort their essence:

- Loving-kindness's near enemy is attachment.
- Compassion's near enemy is pity.
- Joy's near enemy is clinging to pleasant states.
- Equanimity's near enemy is indifference.

True compassion doesn't look down on suffering. It doesn't say, "I feel sorry for you." It says, "I see your pain, and I recognize myself in it." It is intimate, not condescending.

COMPASSION AS SUSTAINABLE CARE

Karuṇā is what allows us to care deeply without burning out. If every time you hear about suffering and you're overwhelmed, that's compassion without equanimity. If you shrug and feel unmoved, that's equanimity without compassion. *Karuṇā* is the middle way: caring deeply while staying steady enough to keep caring tomorrow too.

PRACTICING KARUṆĀ

The training begins with ourselves. We practice recognizing our own suffering, and instead of rejecting or drowning in it, we hold it with warmth. A simple way to practice is with the breath:

"Breathing in, I see the suffering in me."

"Breathing out, I hold it with compassion."

When we can do this for ourselves, it becomes easier to extend it to others. We learn how to be with suffering without being undone by it. That is what *karuṇā* means.

19

FINDING COMPASSION WITHIN

If you find some strong resistance to anything in this chapter, jump to Section III and see if you resonate with those practices.

Some people think compassion is about being soft or being nice. However, when you've lived through trauma or depression, you learn that real compassion is fierce. It has to be.

This chapter is about finding that kind of compassion. Not as a feeling you wait around for, but as a practice you choose.

You already have the capacity for compassion. Every human being does. If you've ever comforted a child, a friend, or an animal who was scared or in pain, you've already felt it. The problem isn't that you're missing compassion. It's that the pathways to it may be buried under exhaustion, fear, or habit.

So we begin by training.

WHY COMPASSION PRACTICE MATTERS

When you send compassion to someone else or to yourself, you're activating something in your brain that the neuroscientist Jaak Panksepp called the Care Circuit. This is the system that evolved in all mammals to soothe distress. It releases oxytocin and other chemicals in the brain that regulate the nervous system and help you feel safe.

This is not imaginary. It's not about living in a fantasy in which everything is fine. It's about activating a physiological system in your brain to regulate distress in your body.

Therefore, we train ourselves to find compassion.

THREE FORMS OF PRACTICE

There are three ways we work with compassion in this chapter:

1. *Sending* compassion to someone else.
2. *Receiving* compassion from someone else.
3. *Sending and receiving*, or letting compassion flow in both directions.

Some people find one style of practice much easier than the others. Experiment with all three, and then use the style that's easiest for you.

SENDING COMPASSION

For many people, *sending* compassion is the easiest way to begin. You picture someone who's easy to love—maybe a pet, a baby, or a dear friend. You offer them a simple wish: that they be well.

This may not seem like much, but it completely changed my life. Try for yourself.

PRACTICE: SENDING COMPASSION

1. Sit in a comfortable position. Let your body settle.
2. Explore different images until you find one that brings up natural and uncomplicated warmth and love. It might be a baby, an animal, or a baby animal. It could be anything at all.
3. Keep that image in your mind. If it's a baby or an animal, you might imagine yourself holding them. Let the image be as clear as possible.
4. Notice any sensations in your body. Do you feel warmth, lightness, or relaxation? Let the feeling be as strong as it wants to be.
5. Experiment with these phrases. Feel free to change them, or drop them if they don't help:
   - "May you be happy."
   - "May you be safe."
   - "May you be loved."
6. As you say these words, notice the sensations in your body now. Let them be as strong as they want to be.
7. Continue for 3–5 minutes.

If it feels good, keep practicing this way. If it feels flat or unreachable, try the next one.

RECEIVING COMPASSION

For some people, sending compassion is challenging, but receiving it can be easier.

The source of the compassion doesn't need to be real. In the same way that watching a horror movie creates a real fear response in your body (elevated heart rate, blood pressure, and adrenaline), just visualizing someone who loves and understands you can create a very real and measurable positive response in your body.

PRACTICE: RECEIVING COMPASSION

1. Find a comfortable posture. Now picture someone or something that you feel could love and understand you, just the way you are. It could be a grandparent, a pet, a tree, or a religious figure. It's okay if they're not real.

2. Imagine them looking at you with kindness.

3. Notice any sensations in your body. Do you feel warmth, lightness, or relaxation? Let the feeling be as strong as it wants to be.

4. Experiment with visualizing them saying these phrases. Feel free to change them, or drop them if they don't help:
   - "May you be happy."
   - "May you be safe."
   - "May you be loved."

5. Let those words land in your body. Allow their compassion into you as deeply as you can, and notice the sensations in your body now. Let them be as strong as they want to be.

You are not forcing yourself to believe these words. You are simply letting them in.

SENDING AND RECEIVING ON THE BREATH

For some people, sending and receiving together is the most powerful practice. As you inhale, receive. As you exhale, send.

Experiment and see how this feels compared to the others.

PRACTICE: SENDING AND RECEIVING

1. Find a comfortable posture. Close your eyes or soften your gaze.
2. Explore different images until you find one that brings up natural and uncomplicated warmth and love. It might be a person, an animal, or anything at all.
3. As you breathe in, silently say, "I receive compassion."
4. As you breathe out, silently say, "I send compassion."
5. Let the breath carry the phrases—no effort, just rhythm.
6. Continue for a few minutes.

If it helps, imagine a visual—a warm light moving in and out or a gentle stream flowing between you.

TROUBLESHOOTING: WHEN COMPASSION FEELS OUT OF REACH

Sometimes you'll try these practices and nothing happens. That's okay. It doesn't mean you're doing it wrong.

If you feel nothing, there might be a part of you that isn't ready for this practice. Skip to Section III and see if the practices there can help you connect with that part.

20

HOLDING SUFFERING WITH COMPASSION

If you find some strong resistance to anything in this chapter, jump to Section III and see if you resonate with those practices.

In Buddhist psychology, all the forms of suffering, including grief, anger, and fear, are seen not as flaws or disorders, but as *seeds* that have been watered by past experiences. Each of us has a storehouse of emotional seeds: joy, sadness, gratitude, fear, wonder, anger. Whether they manifest or stay dormant depends on conditions. If your seed of suffering has been activated, that doesn't mean anything is wrong with you. It means something in your environment, your thoughts, or your memories has watered that seed, and now it's alive in you.

The first step is just to notice it.

When we're caught in suffering, our instinct is often to resist, to shut it down, explain it away, or get rid of it as quickly as possible. However, suffering doesn't respond well to aggression or avoidance. Like a frightened child, it tends to withdraw or act out when met with force, and scream louder when ignored. Healing begins when we're willing to turn toward the suffering with kindness.

That doesn't mean indulging it or wallowing. It means saying, "I see you. I know you're here. I'm not going to abandon you."

Thich Nhat Hanh teaches us to treat our suffering like a crying baby. You don't yell at a baby for crying. You don't tell them to grow up. You pick them up, hold them close, and offer your loving-presence. If the baby feels your warmth, they can begin to settle. Just like that baby, the suffering inside you is asking not to be fixed but to be held.

You don't have to feel ready. You don't have to understand where the suffering is coming from. You only have to be willing to try.

Just for now, invite it to be here.

THE POWER OF LOVING-AWARENESS

The seed of suffering doesn't want to be alone. What it needs is companionship. Not from another person, necessarily, but from the clearest, kindest part of yourself. That part of you is what we call loving-awareness. It's your ability to witness pain without becoming it. It's the gentle inner presence that knows how to stay open.

Loving-awareness is not just a technique. It can be a new way of orienting toward the world. You can think of it like a fragrant flower blooming in the garden of your mind. Wherever it grows it changes the atmosphere. When your seed of suffering meets the presence of loving-awareness, something begins to shift. It might be subtle at first. Just a little more space in your chest or a softening around the eyes, but it matters. This is how transformation begins.

Try saying silently, "I see you, suffering. I am here for you," or

"It's okay to feel this. You don't need to go away." You don't have to mean it completely. Just saying the words begins to make space.

The mind might protest. *This is pointless. This is too much. I can't handle this.* That's okay. You don't have to argue with the mind. The voice that protests is another part of you that is suffering and in need of compassion. Just return to the practice of loving-awareness. You feel the breath. You notice the body. You let the presence in you be bigger than the pain.

Remember: The goal is not to make the suffering disappear. The goal is not to abandon yourself when suffering appears.

With time, you'll find that the suffering becomes less sharp, less overwhelming. It might still be intense, but you'll know how to hold it better, like a parent who no longer panics when the baby cries but instinctively reaches out to comfort them.

COMPOST AND FLOWERS

Thich Nhat Hanh taught that suffering is like garbage. It might not be pleasant, but it can become compost. Then, that compost can be used to grow flowers.

That's not a metaphor to make us feel better. It's a path of practice.

When we treat suffering as something shameful, it festers. When we see how it can feed growth, our relationship with it begins to change. We don't pretend it smells good. We don't pretend we want it, but we respect its potential.

You don't need to believe in the flowers yet. All you need is the willingness to sit beside the compost pile and not run away.

PRACTICE: HOLDING PAIN LIKE A CRYING BABY

When suffering arises, try this:

1. Pause. Take a breath.
2. Notice where you feel the pain. It might be in your chest, your gut, or your throat.
3. Instead of pushing it away, say silently:
   - "I see you, suffering. I'm here for you."
   - "It's okay to feel this. I will take care of you."
4. Place your hand gently over the place where you feel the most pain. Let your hand say what words can't.
5. Stay with the sensation—not the story, just the feeling—for a few more breaths.

If it gets overwhelming, back off. You can turn toward joy for a few minutes, then return later. This is not about enduring. It's about *relating differently* to what's hard.

SUFFERING AS SENSATION

One of the most helpful shifts to learn is to stop seeing suffering as something that's *about* your life—and start seeing it as something that lives in your body. We can learn how to recognize our suffering as sensation in the body, let go of our stories, and embrace it with compassion.

This doesn't mean ignoring your past. It means that transformation doesn't happen in the stories. It happens in the felt experience of holding pain with love.

You can label it "sensation." You can even name the part of you that hates the sensation, and hold *that* part, too: "I feel this heaviness in my chest. And I also feel the part of me that hates how heavy it feels. I'm here for both of you."

FLOWERS YOU'VE ALREADY GROWN

If you've made it this far in life, you've already grown some flowers.

Think of a past struggle, like something you thought you'd never get through. Maybe it still hurts. Yet also, maybe it taught you something. Maybe it gave you more patience, more humility, more compassion for others.

That's what we're doing here. We're taking the compost of life and helping it turn into something fertile. We don't pretend that it smells good, but we see that it makes growth possible.

A BREATH PRACTICE FOR HOLDING SUFFERING

Here's a more structured practice:

1. Sit quietly.

2. With each inhale, say silently: "Breathing in, I acknowledge my suffering."
3. With each exhale: "Breathing out, I send myself love and compassion."
4. Place a hand where you feel the suffering most. Stay for a few minutes.

This is how we retrain the nervous system. We teach it that pain is not dangerous. That the body can feel sadness or fear or grief and still be safe. Over time, this creates real change.

The sharpness fades, and the fear loses its grip. Not because we pushed harder but because we learned to stay present.

SUFFERING CAN BE TRANSFORMED

Not all pain becomes wisdom. Not all suffering becomes compassion. But every moment we choose to stay with our pain in a spirit of love and patience, we create the conditions for that transformation to take place.

Suffering is not a mistake. It's not a punishment. It's part of life's natural cycle, and it can be the raw material from which we grow our deepest strength.

21

TRANSFORMING OLD PAIN

If you find some strong resistance to anything in this chapter, jump to Section III and see if you resonate with those practices.

There are parts of us that feel ancient. Some of the pain we carry is so familiar, so woven into who we are, that it feels permanent. Like nothing could ever touch it.

Yet change is possible. Not because we forget the past, and not because we make peace with it intellectually, but because we learn to hold it differently.

THE 100-YEAR-OLD TREE

If you imagine a 100-year-old tree, you can see that the 50-year-old tree is still present inside it. You can count the rings and point to the exact place where the 10-year-old or 30-year-old tree once lived.

It's the same with us. We carry the entire record of our lives—every experience we've had—etched into the structure of our nervous system. A childhood moment of fear or shame isn't "just in the past." If that experience still affects you today, it's because it still lives in you, like a ring in a tree.

This is why healing the past is possible. You can't change what happened, but you can change the way it lives inside you. You can change the way your nervous system holds that memory. When that happens, the past no longer controls your present.

MEMORY RECONSOLIDATION: HOW CHANGE WORKS

Every time you recall a memory, it becomes unstable and flexible for a short window of time. If during that window you introduce a new experience, especially one that activates the Care Circuit in your brain, then the memory gets rewritten. Not erased, but changed.

This is the neuroscience behind healing trauma, and this is exactly what Buddhist practice has done for centuries: learning to bring love and presence to the places that hurt.

WHAT IT TAKES TO HEAL

There are two ingredients for transforming emotional wounds:

1. Accessing the pain.
2. Bringing compassion into direct contact with it.

Bringing up the pain *without compassion* is rumination. It doesn't help.

Feeling compassion *without touching the pain* feels nice, but doesn't cause deep healing. However, if you can bring both into awareness at the same time, the brain can begin to transform the way that painful experience lives inside you.

GUIDED PRACTICE: THE RINGS OF THE TREE

1. *Settle your body.* Find a quiet space. Let your body be supported. Breathe gently.

2. *Picture yourself as a tree.* A great tree, still and grounded. Imagine each past version of yourself as a ring within the trunk. The 5-year-old. The teenager. The young adult. Each one still present. Each one part of who you are now.

3. *Choose a version of yourself that is still hurting.* Let an image come to mind. Picture your younger self at a time when you felt afraid, humiliated, abandoned, or ashamed. Don't force a dramatic memory; let whatever arises be enough.

4. *Let the pain speak.* What is this younger version of you feeling? What are they believing? Where do you feel it in your body?

5. *Meet them with compassion.* Now imagine the person you are today—wiser, stronger, more resourced—kneeling beside this younger self. Imagine saying:

   "I see you. I know how hard it was. You are not alone. I'm here now."

Or you might say:

"You were always lovable."

1. *Let your hand speak.* Place your hand on your chest, or wherever the sensation is strongest. Let your hand offer reassurance like placing a warm cloth on a wound.
2. *Stay until you feel a shift.* You're not trying to force anything. Just stay with this image and this part of yourself, offering kindness, until you feel some amount of softening.

IF COMPASSION IS HARD TO ACCESS

If it's difficult to feel compassion toward yourself, you can borrow it from an imagined figure. Picture a wise elder, a spiritual teacher, or a loving animal sitting with your younger self. Imagine their voice saying:

"May you be safe."

"May you feel loved."

"You are not alone."

This is not wishful thinking. This is activating the Care Circuit in your brain to heal a painful memory.

22

SELF-COMPASSION IN GOOD TIMES AND BAD

If you find some strong resistance to anything in this chapter, jump to Section III and see if you resonate with those practices.

It's easy to think of self-compassion as something we practice when we're down—when life is hard, we feel rejected, or we're stuck in shame. That's true, but that's not the whole story.

Self-compassion can also be a way of showing up to joy. It can mean letting ourselves feel good without guilt or fear. It can mean receiving love without apology, and allowing ourselves to want what we want without shame.

We need self-compassion *especially* in moments of pain. Yet there is more it can offer.

This chapter is about learning to bring compassion to *all* of it: to moments of conflict, disappointment, and loneliness, as well as to pleasure, excitement, and success.

GUIDED PRACTICE: BEING A FRIEND TO YOURSELF

This practice is a way of training the voice of compassion so it feels natural like a friend you can always turn to:

1. Sit comfortably. Take a few breaths and let your body settle.
2. Bring to mind a recent moment when you felt upset. Not the worst thing, just something that stung a little.
3. Picture yourself in that moment. What did your face look like? Your posture? What were you feeling?
4. Imagine that *someone you love*—a close friend, a child, or even a pet—was the one experiencing what you went through.
5. Ask yourself:
   - o "What would I say to them?"
   - o "What would I want them to know?"

1. Now say those words to yourself. Out loud or silently. Gently. As if you mean them. If you don't know what to say, try:

"May you be safe."

"May you feel loved."

2. Notice how you feel in your body. Allow any sensation to be as strong as it wants to be.

WHEN THINGS GO WRONG: THE THREE STEPS

There's a basic formula I use over and over in my life and in my work with clients. You can apply it to anything from a conflict in your relationship to work stress to a flash of insecurity while scrolling social media.

The steps are simple:

1. Stop.
2. Find the suffering in your body.
3. Send compassion there.

Let's break it down.

1. Stop

When something goes wrong, our first instinct is often to try to react, explain, fix, or distract ourselves. However, in order to find clarity, we have to pause.

Stopping doesn't mean giving up. It means *you notice*. You recognize that something painful has happened, and you choose to meet it instead of avoid it.

2. Find the Suffering in Your Body

Suffering isn't just a story in your head. It's something you might feel in your chest, your gut, your throat, or your face.

Ask yourself: "Where do I feel this? Is it tightness, heat, pressure, hollowness?"

You don't have to name the emotion precisely. Just find the place in your body where it lives. Stay there for a breath or two.

3. Send Compassion There

Now direct compassion right to that part of your body. You can do it with words like:

- "I know this hurts. I'm here with you."
- "It's okay to feel this. You're not alone."
- "May you feel loved. May you feel supported."

You might also place a hand over your heart or on your belly. Breathe into the sensation, and let your body know: *You're safe now. I'm not abandoning you.*

This three-step process can take less than a minute or it can unfold over several minutes. You can use it when you get bad news, after a conflict, or when you notice yourself falling into an old pattern.

It works by retraining your nervous system to know that suffering is not dangerous, and that love is available, even now.

VISUALIZING MOMENTS OF DISAPPOINTMENT

Let's take an example: You didn't get a job you really wanted.

The mind may start with *I'm not good enough. I'll never get anywhere. I shouldn't have even applied.*

Instead of arguing with those thoughts, stop:

- Picture the moment you found out.
- Where did you feel it? Maybe a pit in your stomach.
- Place your hand there. Imagine someone kind sitting beside you saying, "This hurts. That makes sense to me. I know how much you wanted this. I'm here with you."

Now breathe. That's the practice. It's not about erasing pain. It's about staying human in the middle of it.

APPLYING IT TO RELATIONSHIPS

Maybe someone said something that hurt you. Maybe you're angry or you're blaming yourself.

Before you react, go inward:

- Stop.
- Find the pain in your body.
- Hold it like a crying child.

Let compassion hold your pain. Then, once you're steady, decide what to say or do.

GOOD TIMES TOO

When life feels good, we sometimes recoil. We worry it won't last, or we think we don't deserve it. That's where self-compassion can show up again.

Try saying:

- "It's okay to feel happy."
- "You deserve good things, just like everyone else."
- "You don't need to apologize for joy."

Receiving joy is just as important as surviving hardship. Self-compassion helps with both.

IN EVERY MOMENT

Whatever you're facing—grief, confusion, fear, celebration—the path is the same:

1. Stop.
2. Find the suffering (or joy) in your body.
3. Send compassion.

This is what makes self-compassion a life practice. Not a trick or a technique. It's a relationship with yourself that gets stronger every time you come home to it.

23

THE INNER CRITIC NEEDS COMPASSION

If you find some strong resistance to anything in this chapter, jump to Section III and see if you resonate with those practices.

When we begin to practice self-compassion, one of the first things many people notice is how quickly something inside them pushes back.

You sit down to breathe, or to offer yourself kindness, and a voice comes in—sharp, cold, familiar:

"You don't deserve this."

"This won't help."

"Who do you think you are?"

That's your inner critic. If you're like most people, it's been with you a long time.

A PART OF YOU, NOT THE WHOLE OF YOU

The inner critic often sounds like the truth, but it's not. It's a part of you that formed to try to keep you safe.

Maybe it believes that if it's hard enough on you, you'll stop making mistakes. Maybe it thinks shame will protect you from being hurt again. Maybe it learned, early on, that being kind to yourself was dangerous.

However it formed, it came from pain, and it's made out of pain. That's why it hurts so much to hear it.

NOT AN ENEMY—A WOUND

In Buddhist practice, we learn to stop treating parts of ourselves like enemies. That includes the critic.

The inner critic is not evil. It's not "the bad voice." It's a wounded part of you that thinks harshness is the only thing keeping you from falling apart. In that way, it's trying to help.

That doesn't mean you have to agree with it, or obey it. It does mean that yelling back or trying to shut it down usually doesn't work.

The critic doesn't need more punishment. Like every form of suffering, it needs compassion. Even if that's the last thing it would ever ask for.

YOU DON'T HAVE TO BE READY YET

If this idea feels difficult, that's okay. You don't have to fix anything today. You don't even have to agree. Just see if you can hold the possibility that this voice—the one that attacks you when you're down—might be a part of you that's scared, tired, or a part that's been trying to carry something heavy for a very long time.

If you can hold that possibility, you've already started to change your relationship with it.

YOU'LL COME BACK TO THIS

For many people, the inner critic is one of the strongest obstacles to healing. That's why the entire third section of this book is devoted to working with it.

If compassion feels out of reach because something inside you keeps pushing it away, that section will help. You'll learn how to work with resistance gently, how to understand your internal blocks, and how to shift the critic's role in your life without force or judgment.

For now, all you need to know is this: The inner critic is made of suffering, and like all suffering, it needs compassion.

24

CULTIVATING EQUANIMITY

If you find some strong resistance to anything in this chapter, jump to Section III and see if you resonate with those practices.

Equanimity is not the same as indifference. It's not resignation, and it's not giving up. Equanimity is what allows us to care *without being overwhelmed*. It allows us to feel the full weight of joy and sorrow, and hope and despair, without collapsing under them.

When you're struggling with depression, people often tell you to "stop worrying," or "don't take things personally." However, equanimity doesn't come from trying to feel less. It comes from expanding your capacity to be with what's already here.

In Buddhist psychology, equanimity (*upekkhā*) is one of the four *brahmavihāras*, or "divine abodes." Thich Nhat Hanh has sometimes translated it as inclusiveness, the ability to be open to all of your experience with a steady heart. Not because you're numb, but because you're rooted. Your nervous system is grounded enough that you don't need to run away. Your mind is clear enough that you can see causes and conditions. Your heart is wide enough that you can love what's imperfect without needing to control it.

When you're in pain, it's natural to want to change your

experience—to push away the bad and chase the good. Yet pain is an inevitable part of life, and our aversion to it often makes it worse. We learn to enjoy moments of happiness and to bring love to moments of suffering. Therefore, we don't have to run away from anything.

Equanimity is what makes compassion sustainable. Without it, we either burn out or shut down. With it, we can keep our hearts open, even when the world is breaking.

This chapter is about learning how to do that.

THE WORLD IS NOT WHAT WE WANTED

One of the hallmarks of depression is rigidity. It's a mind that insists that *this is not okay*. There's injustice, grief, failure, loneliness. There are parts of yourself you might have labeled as *unacceptable*, and part of you might still feel attached to that view. You might even think that calling something unacceptable is how you make it better.

Equanimity doesn't mean pretending that bad things are good. It means being open to what's here.

It means trusting that *being open* is more beneficial than staying closed.

UPEKKHĀ IS NOT COLD

Equanimity only works if it includes compassion. Otherwise, it becomes detachment or apathy. If you say "everything is fine" while someone is suffering—including yourself—that's not *upekkhā*. That's avoidance.

True equanimity means saying, "This is painful. I care deeply. And bringing love to suffering is what gives life meaning."

We can feel both openness and care, because we don't have the naive expectation that the world will stop having bad things. We don't want bad things to happen, but we know that they will, and we know it's okay. It gives us the opportunity to grow our compassion.

SEEING THE WHOLE PICTURE

Thich Nhat Hanh taught that in every moment there are infinite reasons to suffer and infinite reasons to be grateful. What matters is where we place our attention.

He never meant that as a way to bypass pain. He meant that the world is always more than whatever story we're caught in. Depression flattens reality. Equanimity restores dimension.

You can hold suffering *and* beauty in the same breath. You can say *yes* to the world, not because it always feels good, but because that's the only place healing can happen.

TRUSTING WHAT YOU CAN'T CONTROL

Part of cultivating equanimity is learning to trust things you can't control. That trust may never feel easy, but it's a skill we can practice.

The Tibetan tradition teaches that the human realm, with its mix of joy and suffering, is *just right* for awakening. Not because everything's fine, but because there is just the right amount of suffering to teach us what we most need to learn. Beings born into a hell realm have too much suffering to practice, and beings born into a divine deva realm get everything they want immediately, so they never have a chance to develop patience, compassion, or any kind of virtue. In this teaching, the human realm gives us enough pain that we are forced to grow, but no more.

The 17th-century philosopher Gottfried Leibniz once said that we live in "the best of all possible worlds." Not because this world is perfect, but because it's the only one in which freedom and compassion can develop.

You don't have to believe that. You only have to be willing to see what becomes possible when you stop trying to control the uncontrollable.

PRACTICE: NAMING WHAT'S HERE

One simple way to train equanimity is to sit quietly and name whatever is present in your experience: pleasant, unpleasant, or neutral. Not to change it. Just to see it:

1. Sit in stillness for a few breaths.
2. Begin to note:
    - *Pleasant*: warmth in the sun, a memory, soft clothing.
    - *Unpleasant*: tightness in your stomach, fatigue, judgment.
    - *Neutral*: sounds, thoughts, background sensations.
3. Notice your reactions: craving, aversion, numbness. Don't fight them.
4. Say silently, "It's okay for this to be here too."

Even the part of you that wishes it were different, that too is welcome.

EQUANIMITY IS FREEDOM

The more you practice, the more space opens up. It's not that the world changes, but that *you* do. You stop needing to hold your breath until things go your way. You stop needing to brace against what you can't fix.

Equanimity doesn't make you passive. It makes you stable, clear, and responsive. It lets you care deeply about what matters *without being broken* by what you can't control.

This is not the kind of freedom that floats above life. It's the kind that moves through it with grounded strength.

Try saying to yourself:

"Today, I am learning to stay present with what is."

"I will not label this moment as wrong."

"I will meet the world with openness and care."

This is the heart of equanimity: the ability to say *yes*, even though things aren't the way you want them to be. Things are the way they are, and the *world as it is* is sacred.

25

RIGHT VIEW AND INTERBEING

If you find some strong resistance to anything in this chapter, jump to Section III and see if you resonate with those practices.

When we're depressed, our view of ourselves and the world often becomes distorted. We see suffering as personal failure. We believe that we're alone in our pain. The Buddhist teaching of Right View can help undo that illusion. It shows us that suffering is never just personal. It's the result of many causes and conditions, most of which we didn't choose. This shift isn't about blaming others. It's about stepping out of blame altogether. Right View is one of the most fundamental aspects of Buddhist practice, and the key to the type of understanding that can liberate us.

NOTHING EXISTS ALONE

One of the deepest expressions of Right View is the teaching of *interbeing*. Thich Nhat Hanh coined this term to help us understand the truth of nonseparation. He would often say, "The piece of paper you are holding is made entirely of nonpaper elements."

If you look deeply into a sheet of paper, you can see the tree that it came from. In our normal way of thinking, we might say that the tree is gone. However, it's possible to see that the tree is still present in the paper. The tree hasn't disappeared. It has transformed into paper. If you try to remove the tree from the paper, there is nothing left. If you can get yourself to see things this way, it can radically change what feels possible.

Let's look a little deeper in the paper. You can see the sunshine and rain that helped the tree grow are also present. You can see the logger who cut it, the factory worker who processed it, the ancestors of those people, the food they ate, the earth they all came from. If you remove any of those elements, the paper couldn't exist. So we say the paper cannot *be* on its own—it must *inter-be* with everything else. It is made entirely of nonpaper elements.

This is true for us too. Every molecule in your body has been part of the earth, the sky, and the food chain for millions of years. Think of one water molecule in your blood. How long has that been a water molecule? Before being part of your blood, it might have been tea in a cup. Before that, it might have been in a reservoir. Looking back further, it has been rain, clouds, and part of every ocean. It was a water molecule when the earth formed, and now it's part of you.

Every idea in your mind was shaped by generations of conversations, experiences, and cultural stories. You are not a separate self. You are a process made of relationships. You inter-are with everything.

HOW THIS CHANGES SUFFERING

When we're caught in pain, especially emotional pain, it feels like we *are the pain*. As if it defines us. Buddhism teaches that the self is not a fixed thing. It's an unfolding, interconnected stream of causes and conditions. Like the paper, our pain is made entirely of non-self elements.

That means your suffering is not a verdict. It's not who you are. It's part of a much larger process: your family, your society, your history. If suffering has causes, it also has conditions that can allow it to transform. You are not stuck:

- When we understand interbeing, we stop thinking of self-compassion and compassion for others as separate things.
- If everything is interconnected, then the care we give ourselves ripples outward.
- By tending to our own suffering, we create the conditions for more peace in the world around us.

This is Right View. It sees that the suffering in you is not just *yours*. Your healing is not just *for you*.

THERE IS NO ONE TO BLAME

Without Right View, we fall into what Thich Nhat Hanh called "wrong mindfulness." We use our practice to try to improve ourselves in isolation, trying to become acceptable, trying to get rid of what we think is wrong with us.

With Right View, we stop looking for someone to blame. Not ourselves. Not our parents. Not even the people who hurt us. Instead, we start to understand that everyone is shaped by conditions:

> Your anxiety might come from your mother's anxiety. Hers might come from growing up without enough food, or from her grandfather's trauma in a war.
>
> The suffering of the world belongs to all of us, and we all share responsibility for transforming it.

This insight doesn't erase accountability. It just means we stop pretending that suffering begins and ends with individuals. We see the web of interbeing, and that vision makes compassion possible.

INTERBEING IS THE FOUNDATION OF HEALING

Trauma isolates us. It tells us our pain is unique, or our fault, or proof that we don't belong. But interbeing shows us something different: that we are always already connected.

The suffering in you touches the suffering in others. Your healing creates conditions for the healing of others. Every act of compassion you offer yourself is part of a much bigger story:

- When we heal, we do not heal just for ourselves.

- Our healing impacts our relationships, our communities, and even future generations.
- Healing is an act of interbeing.

PRACTICE: SEEING THE CAUSES AND CONDITIONS

When you're caught in pain, try this:

1. *Pause*: Feel your breath.
2. *Say silently*: "This pain did not begin with me. It was transmitted to me."
3. *Ask*: "Who transmitted their suffering to me? Who had transmitted it to them?"
4. *Know*: "Someone will need to hold this suffering with compassion for it to heal."

You may begin to see your pain as part of something larger. You may start to soften. That's enough.

26

THE INTERGENERATIONAL FACTORY OF LIFE

If you find some strong resistance to anything in this chapter, jump to Section III and see if you resonate with those practices.

One of the ways that I visualize interbeing is to picture that each of us is a worker in a great factory, a factory that produces the complex beauty of life.

We all stand along a conveyor belt that never stops moving. On this conveyor belt, we receive transmissions from every generation that came before us. They show up in our bodies, our thoughts, our relationships, and our worldview. These transmissions are everything that make up our experience.

THE BEAUTY WE INHERIT

Sometimes, the conveyor belt brings us a flower. That flower might be anything that you like about yourself: the color of your eyes, your ability to appreciate music, or the love you have for children. It might be resilience, creativity, compassion, or strength.

When a flower comes down the belt, our job is simple. We just need to appreciate it and let it nourish us. If we ignore it, if we get too busy, too self-important, or too consumed by comparison, then it begins to wilt. The joy it could have given us fades.

You didn't grow that flower. It was grown by the lives of those who came before you. If you're lucky enough to receive it, your only job is to recognize its beauty and allow it to feed your life.

THE SUFFERING WE INHERIT

More often, what shows up on the conveyor belt is a big pile of suffering. Sometimes it's anger, shame, or anxiety. Sometimes it's a deep fear of abandonment. Sometimes it's bitterness, judgment, or despair.

It's the suffering of past generations. It's their unhealed wounds arriving in your life completely uninvited.

Your job, when a pile of suffering arrives, is not to panic. It's not to run away or push it down the line to someone else. Your job is to meet it with compassion.

That's what transforms it.

THE WAND OF COMPASSION

You are holding a wand made of compassion. When suffering arrives, you don't have to fix it. You only have to touch it with your compassion.

If you can do that, the suffering will begin to change. Right before your eyes, the pile of suffering begins to decompose.

It becomes compost, and compost, if treated with care, can someday grow a flower.

This is how suffering becomes compassion, and how compassion can become joy.

EVERYTHING IS A TRANSMISSION

There is nothing about you—nothing you like about yourself and nothing you hate—that began with you. Every beautiful and terrible thing in your life is a transmission. It came from somewhere: your ancestors, your community, your culture, your biology, your environment.

This is the teaching of interbeing. You do not exist separately from the world. You are made of relationships, stories, sunshine, and soil.

You are not defined by what you've inherited. However, you are responsible for how you respond to it.

THE WORK OF A LIFETIME

There is no finish line. The conveyor belt keeps moving. More suffering will come. More flowers will come. Your job is the same: Receive the beauty with appreciation. Meet the suffering with compassion.

Sometimes, the piles are so big and so awful that it's overwhelming. Sometimes you feel like you're the only one receiving them. That's not true. Everyone is handed suffering. Everyone passes some of it along. You are not alone.

If you can meet even one pile of suffering with compassion, you've changed the pattern. You've created a small break in the cycle, and that break can grow.

PRACTICE: TOUCH AND TRANSFORM

1. Sit in stillness. Breathe.
2. Bring to mind a difficult pattern in yourself—something painful or destructive.
3. Ask: "Where did this suffering come from? Who passed it to me?"
4. Say silently: "This suffering did not start with me, but I have the opportunity to hold it differently."
5. Imagine touching that suffering with your wand of compassion.

That's all you have to do.

THIS IS INTERBEING

Right View means knowing that nothing exists alone. Your joy, your pain, your strengths, your fears—none of them are yours in isolation. You inter-are with all of it.

You are not separate from the causes of your suffering. You are not separate from the beauty that sustains you.

We all stand at the same conveyor belt. We all hold the same responsibility.

None of us are doing this alone.

27

TRAINING THE MIND WITH THE EIGHTFOLD PATH

If you find some strong resistance to anything in this chapter, jump to Section III and see if you resonate with those practices.

The Buddha taught that liberation comes from training the mind. We have the opportunity to choose qualities that we want to grow in ourselves. We can choose to grow our steadiness, clarity, compassion, and wisdom, so that we can meet life as it is, and respond in ways that reduce suffering. The Eightfold Path is the most complete framework the Buddha gave for how to do that.

WHY THIS MATTERS NOW

When we're depressed, anxious, or caught in shame, we don't just feel bad. We start to see the world through a distorted lens. Our thoughts become rigid, our energy disappears, and our relationships suffer.

Training the mind is what allows us to relate differently to those states. Not by forcing change, but by slowly building the conditions that allow clarity and compassion to arise.

The Eightfold Path gives us the architecture for that change.

THE EIGHTFOLD PATH

The Eightfold Path is traditionally divided into three areas: wisdom, ethical conduct, and mental discipline. They all work together to support the training of the heart and mind.

1. Right View

Seeing life clearly. Understanding that everything arises from causes and conditions, including our suffering. When we stop blaming ourselves or others, compassion becomes possible.

Right View is grounded in *interbeing*: The insight that nothing exists alone. Every thought, emotion, and reaction comes from somewhere. If we can see that clearly, we stop taking everything so personally, and we begin to open.

2. Right Intention

Choosing to meet life with kindness, compassion, and the willingness to let go of what causes suffering.

This is where you say, "I don't have to keep hurting myself. I want to relate to my pain with more love."

Right Intention sets the direction of our practice. Even on the days when we can't follow through, just remembering our deepest intention is already a step toward healing.

3. Right Speech

We learn to speak in such a way that contributes to self-confidence, joy, and hope in ourselves and in the other person.

What tone do you use with yourself when you're struggling? Right Speech asks, "What would it be like to speak to myself the way I would to a beloved friend?"

4. Right Action

Living in ways that reduce harm and reflect our values. This can mean how we treat others, but it also includes things like resting when we're exhausted, or choosing to reach out when we need connection.

Right Action isn't about perfection. It's just the action that arises naturally from Right View, Right Intention, and Right Speech.

5. Right Livelihood

Engaging in work that doesn't cause harm and supports well-being. For some people, this is about employment. For others, it's about how we use our time, attention, and energy.

This path includes asking, "Where am I directing my energy each day? Who and what do I serve?"

6. Right Effort

When we've started to experience the benefits of practice, it gives rise to a natural desire to practice more. We nurture what is wholesome, which is anything that contributes to our long-term well-being. We gently let go of what is unwholesome, which is anything that causes suffering:

There is a seed of despair in you.

But there is also a seed of joy, a seed of love, and a seed of peace.

Which seed will you water today?

Right Effort doesn't mean trying harder. It means remembering the benefits of practice and tending the seeds you want to grow.

7. Right Mindfulness

Bringing kind, clear awareness to what is happening in the present moment without clinging, without pushing away.

Right Mindfulness is not neutral. It's not merely observing things for no reason. It's awareness with care. It asks, "Can I notice what's happening in my body and heart with enough space to choose how I respond?"

This is the skill that allows us to hold suffering without being consumed by it.

8. Right Concentration

The ability to stabilize the mind, gather our scattered attention, and rest it on something healing.

This isn't about perfect focus. It's about creating space in the mind so that insight, compassion, and steadiness can grow. Even just following the breath for a few minutes each day begins to build this capacity. And Right Concentration leads back to Right View by helping us to see the world more clearly.

TRAINING THE MIND GENTLY

Each of these paths is a doorway. You don't have to walk through all of them at once. Some days, you might just work with Right Effort: choosing to water the seed of kindness instead of self-judgment. Other days, you might return to Right View: remembering that nothing you're feeling exists in isolation.

The point is not to be perfect. The point is to train the mind in a new direction—toward clarity, compassion, and freedom.

A PRACTICE TO BEGIN

At the start of each day, you might pause and ask:

- "What part of the path will I practice today?"
- "Where is suffering showing up in my life, and how might I meet it differently?"
- "What would it mean to practice Right View, Right Speech, or Right Mindfulness right now?"

These are small questions, but if you ask them often, they begin to reshape your whole life.

28

THE DISCOURSE ON LOVE

If you find some strong resistance to anything in this chapter, jump to Section III and see if you resonate with those practices.

Some teachings are so beautiful, so complete, that simply reading them is an act of practice. The *Discourse on Love*, or *Metta Sutta*, is one of them.

If you've read this far, you've already explored many of its teachings. We've spent time with compassion, equanimity, joy, and mindfulness. We've trained ourselves to turn toward suffering with love, to see joy as a source of strength, to water the seeds we want to grow.

This chapter is a chance to step back and receive the whole teaching as a single body of wisdom. The *Metta Sutta* is not just a poem. It's a map for becoming a refuge, for ourselves and for others.

LOVE AS A MIND STATE, NOT A FEELING

In English, we sometimes think of "love" as a kind of sentiment, like a warm, affectionate emotion. But in Buddhist practice, love (*mettā*) is a deliberate, trainable state of mind.

It's not something you wait to feel. It's something you generate.

Mettā is the intention to bring happiness to yourself and others. It's the wish that all beings be safe, joyful, and free. That includes people you like and people you don't like. It includes yourself on your best day, and on the day you didn't get out of bed.

When you hear the word "love" in this chapter, don't think about romance. Think about stability. Think about a mountain of kindness that doesn't move when the weather changes.

THE FOUR QUALITIES OF BOUNDLESS LOVE

The *Metta Sutta* teaches four aspects of true love, known as the *brahmavihāras*, or "divine abodes." These qualities support and balance one another. They are not separate practices. They are one state of mind expressing itself in different directions:

1. *Mettā*—the wish for happiness. You want yourself and others to be well. Not because they earned it. Just because they are alive.

2. *Karuṇā*—compassion. You don't want others to suffer. You see pain, and your heart responds with tenderness.

3. *Muditā*—joy. When someone else is happy, you feel glad. Their happiness uplifts you, not threatens you.

4. *Upekkhā*—equanimity. You know that all things arise and pass away. You care deeply, but without clinging or aversion.

You may notice that we've explored each of these qualities throughout this book. The *Metta Sutta* brings them together into one luminous whole.

A MIND LIKE A MOTHER

Here is my own translation of the discourse:

May all people be happy and safe, and may every heart be filled with joy.

May all beings live in peace and security—whether they are strong or weak, tall or short, large or small, whether seen or unseen, near or far, already born or yet to be born. May every one of them dwell in deep serenity.

Let no one harm another. Let no one endanger the life of another being. Let no one, driven by anger or hatred, wish suffering upon anyone.

Just as a mother would guard her only child with her life, let us cultivate a love that knows no bounds, and offer it to every living being throughout the cosmos.

Let this limitless love fill the entire universe—in every direction, above and below, across every distance. May our love meet no resistance. May our hearts be free from hatred and division. Whether we are standing or walking, sitting or lying down, as long as we are awake, let us keep this love alive in our hearts. This is the most noble way to live.

Freed from confusion, craving, and attachment, living with grace and clarity, those who embody boundless love will surely move beyond birth and death.

Reading these words, what sensations do you notice in your body?

A PRACTICE TO BEGIN

You can try this simple meditation, inspired by the *Metta Sutta*:

Sit quietly. Let your breathing settle.

Then silently say:

- "May I be safe."
- "May I be peaceful."
- "May I be joyful."
- "May I live with ease."

You don't have to believe the words. Just offer them like a gentle hand.

After a few minutes, bring someone else to mind—a friend, a loved one:

- "May you be safe."
- "May you be peaceful."
- "May you be joyful."
- "May you live with ease."

Then try someone neutral. Then someone difficult. Then, if you're ready, all beings:

- "May all beings be safe."
- "May all beings be peaceful."
- "May all beings be joyful."
- "May all beings live with ease."

LOVE WITHOUT EXCLUSION

The *Discourse on Love* teaches that it's possible to love with no boundary. We don't need to draw a line around who deserves kindness and who doesn't. Not even ourselves.

It's easy to fall into a mindset of exclusion. *I can care about everyone except that person. I can be compassionate except on days like today. I can love myself except when I fail.*

This practice asks *What happens when you include even that*?

Even your doubt. Even your fatigue. Even the person you can't forgive.

29

THE BETTER WAY TO LIVE ALONE

If you find some strong resistance to anything in this chapter, jump to Section III and see if you resonate with those practices.

There's a story Thich Nhat Hanh used to tell about this sutra. One day, a group of monks came to the Buddha with a question. They told him about a monk in their community who didn't speak to anyone. He took his meals alone. He didn't participate in the *sangha*. He meditated by himself in the forest and refused to interact.

The monks wanted to know if that was that the right way to live.

The Buddha answered with what we now call the *Bhaddekaratta Sutta*, or the *Better Way to Live Alone*.

NOT SOLITUDE, BUT FREEDOM

The Buddha didn't say this monk was wrong for being alone in the forest. Instead, he made a deeper point: True freedom has nothing to do with how many people are around you. It has to do with your relationship to your own mind.

He said:

"Do not pursue the past.

Do not lose yourself in the future.

The past no longer is.

The future has not yet come.

Look deeply at life as it is in the very here and now,

and dwell in freedom.

The sage calls a person who

dwells in mindfulness

night and day

'the one who knows the better way to live alone.'"

To live alone in the way the Buddha taught means to live untangled. It means to live in this moment—not bound by memory, not pulled by fear. It means you don't need to run.

LIVING WITH GHOSTS

Most of us don't live that way.

We live surrounded by old arguments, unfinished conversations, shame from 10 years ago. We live in a blur of planning and worry, running through scenarios like a movie we can't stop.

When we're depressed, this gets worse. We might spend hours reliving what went wrong or imagining every way the future might fall apart. We become haunted by stories that aren't happening anymore, and might never happen at all.

The mind that lives this way is never really alone. It's never at peace.

COMING HOME TO THE PRESENT

The Better Way to Live Alone is an invitation to return to the only place where healing is possible: the present.

That doesn't mean we forget the past. It means we stop living inside it. It doesn't mean we stop caring about the future. It means we don't lose ourselves in those thoughts.

Thich Nhat Hanh often said, "This moment is a teacher." If we can come back to what's actually happening—our breath, our body, the sensations and feelings of now—we stop resisting life. That's when our heart can open.

A PRACTICE FROM THE SUTTA

You can try this practice:

Sit quietly. Place your hand on your chest or your belly.

Say silently:

- "Breathing in, I let go of the past."
- "Breathing out, I release the future."

- "Breathing in, I arrive in this moment."
- "Breathing out, I feel at home."

You don't have to stop your thoughts. Just realize that they are thoughts. Let them float by like leaves on a stream, and come back to what's real.

WHEN THE MOMENT FEELS UNBEARABLE

Some moments are too painful to live in directly. When you're overwhelmed or despairing, the present can feel like the last place you want to be. That's okay.

This practice is not to force yourself into stillness. It's to make gentle contact with the now. One breath. One footstep. One sound.

The key is to come home slowly, without violence. To remember that the present moment is not trying to punish you. It's trying to welcome you back.

LIVING ALONE AS LIBERATION

The monk in the forest might have looked like he was living alone. Yet if he was caught in anger or pride, he wasn't free. The monks who came to the Buddha might have looked connected, but if they were caught in judgment or comparison, they weren't free either.

Freedom doesn't depend on circumstances. It depends on how you relate to the present.

The Better Way to Live Alone is not about cutting yourself off from others. It's about connecting with reality. It's about dwelling in the only place you can truly be alive.

Let this moment be enough. Let this breath carry you home.

30

THE SECOND ARROW

If you find some strong resistance to anything in this chapter, jump to Section III and see if you resonate with those practices.

The Buddha was teaching a group of monks and he asked them, "If a person is shot by an arrow, would it hurt?"

The monks said, "Yes, Lord. It would."

Then the Buddha asked, "And if they were shot again, in the same place, by a second arrow, would it hurt more?"

The monks replied, "Yes. It would hurt a hundred times more."

The Buddha said, "That is what we do to ourselves."

THE FIRST ARROW

The first arrow is what life throws at you: loss, illness, loneliness, or rejection. Someone you love says something cruel, or a plan you were counting on falls apart. You wake up feeling completely empty for no reason you can name.

That's the inevitable pain of life. You didn't choose it. You don't have to like it, but it happens to everyone.

The first arrow is the pain you can't avoid.

THE SECOND ARROW

The second arrow can be the story you tell about the pain:

"I'm such an idiot for getting my hopes up."

"This always happens. Nothing ever works out."

"I'm broken."

"I shouldn't be feeling this way."

"Everyone else is doing better than me."

The second arrow might also be how you react to the pain in your body. Tensing around it, bracing, shutting down, or distracting yourself in ways that create more suffering.

You shoot the second arrow because you're trying to protect yourself. But it doesn't protect you. It hurts a hundred times worse.

LEARNING TO STOP AFTER THE FIRST ARROW

Mindfulness practice is about learning to stop at the first arrow.

You feel pain.

You pause.

You breathe.

You say, "This hurts. This is what pain feels like. This is enough."

That moment—before the second arrow flies—is where your freedom lives.

You don't have to shoot it. Even if you already have, you don't have to shoot a third.

PRACTICE: STAYING WITH THE FIRST ARROW

Next time something hurts, try this:

1. Stop.
2. Place your hand on your body—wherever you feel the pain most clearly.
3. Say silently, "This is the first arrow."
4. Let your body breathe. Let your mind soften. Don't add anything. Just stay.

If thoughts come up—blame, shame, what-if stories—acknowledge them gently. Then return to your breath, your body, and the part of you that just needs to be held.

WHY WE REACH FOR THE SECOND ARROW

The second arrow can feel like control. Like if we can just figure out what went wrong—who to blame, what to fix—we'll be safe:

Sometimes it feels like punishment. Like if we hurt ourselves first, no one else can.

Sometimes it's just a habit.

The Buddha wasn't blaming us for reacting. He was showing us that we have a choice. That we can stop adding to our own pain.

That we can be on our own side.

COMPASSION IS WHAT HEALS THE FIRST ARROW

The Buddha taught that you don't need to resist pain. You just need to hold it with tenderness:

You don't need to have the right words. Just a breath and just presence.

The first arrow is already hard enough. You don't need to make it worse.

That's the heart of the practice:

Stay with the first arrow.
Don't pick up the bow.
Place your hand on your heart and say,
"This hurts, and I will not abandon myself."

31

YOU HAVE NO COWS TO LOSE

If you find some strong resistance to anything in this chapter, jump to Section III and see if you resonate with those practices.

One day, the Buddha and a group of monks were resting and eating in the forest when a frantic farmer ran up to them. His face was streaked with sweat and dirt. His clothes were torn. He was trembling.

He cried out, "Please, have you seen my cows? I had 12. They broke through the fence and ran off. I've looked everywhere. Without them, I have nothing. If I don't find them, I might as well die."

The Buddha answered gently, "No. I'm sorry but we haven't seen your cows. Try looking in another direction."

After the man disappeared into the trees, still shouting their names, the Buddha turned to his students. He smiled and said, "Dear friends, you are very lucky. You have no cows to lose."

WHAT ARE YOUR COWS?

Thich Nhat Hanh told this story often. He would pause after the Buddha's punchline, smile at the audience and ask, "What are your cows?"

It's a simple story, but if you let it sink in, it reveals something profound.

Your "cows" are whatever you think you can't live without. They might be your job. Your status. Your appearance. Your success. The way other people see you. The idea that you should have been further along by now. The belief that you're only worthy if you're producing, pleasing, achieving.

We all have them.

When they disappear or when we think they might, we panic. Like the farmer, we run around in circles trying to get them back, convinced that if we lose them, our lives are over.

THE DIFFERENCE BETWEEN LOSING AND LETTING GO

Here's the truth: You are going to lose some of your cows.

Everything you cling to, and everything you think defines you, will eventually change or fall away. That's not personal. That's life.

There's a big difference between losing your cows and letting them go.

Either way, you end up with no cows. However, one is excruciating, and the other is liberating.

Losing feels like collapse. Letting go feels like freedom.

WHEN DEPRESSION IS THE EMPTY FIELD

If you're experiencing depression, it might feel like your cows are already gone. Your energy. Your motivation. Your sense of meaning. You might look out at your life and see only the empty field.

It's easy to confuse that emptiness with failure.

What if this isn't failure? What if this is the moment before freedom?

What if, instead of chasing after what used to define you, you could stop and ask, "What if I just let go of everything I believe I can't live without? I don't need to chase anything away, but I can realize life and beauty are still available."

PRACTICE: NAMING YOUR COWS

Sit for a few moments. Bring your awareness to your breath.

Then ask yourself:

- "What am I afraid to lose?"
- "What am I afraid already *has* been lost?"
- "What would it mean to stop chasing it?"

Try naming your cows—not to judge them, but to see them clearly.

You might find that one of your cows is a relationship, your self-image, or the belief that healing should be faster than it is.

Notice which ones make your chest tighten. Which ones have you been chasing even in your sleep?

Then ask, "What would happen if I let them go?"

LETTING GO DOESN'T MEAN YOU DON'T CARE

Letting go is not the same as not loving. You can love someone deeply and still release the belief that they're the only path to your happiness. You can pursue a dream with your whole heart and still know that it doesn't define your worth.

Letting go doesn't mean chasing something away. It means that it can come or go on its own.

It means trusting that your happiness isn't dependent on conditions lining up a certain way.

It means resting in something deeper than outcomes.

YOU ALREADY KNOW THIS

At some point, your life has taught you this lesson. There's something you thought you couldn't survive, and then you did.

Maybe it broke you for a while, and maybe you're still healing.

But you're here.

That means there's already a seed in you that knows how to stop running. That knows how to sit in the middle of the field and say, "The cows are gone, and I'm still here. I'm still breathing. Maybe I don't need them as much as I thought."

When you hear the Buddha say, "You are very lucky. You have no cows to lose," he's not laughing at the farmer. He's not above suffering. He's showing us a path out of it.

Because it's not the cows that cause our pain. It's the chasing.

SECTION III

TRANSFORMING OBSTACLES *to* CHANGE

32

PARTS IN CONFLICT: UNDERSTANDING COMPETING COMMITMENTS

WORKING WITH COMPETING COMMITMENTS

If you're reading this section, it may be because you noticed something important: resistance. Perhaps you were practicing one of the earlier exercises and, instead of feeling supported, you felt a wall inside yourself. Maybe you thought, "This doesn't feel right," or "I just can't make myself do this."

If that happened, you're in the right place. This section was written specifically for you. That's because resistance is not a detour from our practice. It *is* our practice.

Some readers may have found a few practices helpful before encountering resistance. Others might have felt resistance almost immediately, and skipped here after only a chapter or two. Both experiences are perfectly normal. Everyone who works with depression eventually encounters inner resistance, and it is one of the most important gateways to healing.

What you're experiencing is not laziness, lack of discipline, or a flaw in your character. Resistance is the voice of a part of you that's trying to protect you. In Western psychology, we can call these dynamics *competing commitments*. In Buddhist language, they're *samskaras* or "habit-energies"—patterns that once helped you survive but now keep you stuck. When one part of you longs for healing and another part pulls away, it creates the feeling of ambivalence, procrastination, or even outright rejection of the practices you know could help.

This section will help you understand those inner conflicts, identify your own competing commitments, and learn to transform the suffering at its core. Instead of pushing past resistance, we'll we turn toward it with compassion. You'll discover that the parts of you that hold back are not enemies but guardians carrying old pain. With care, they can be heard, understood, and eventually transformed into allies on the path of healing.

Sometimes we feel stuck. We know what would help or at least what might be beneficial, but something inside resists. Sometimes, you might set the intention to be kind to yourself, and another voice says, "That's weak." You might long for connection, and another part of you withdraws in fear. You might think about the positive conditions in your life, but then you hear "Don't get too comfortable. Something bad will happen."

This can feel like sabotage, as though some secret enemy is working against you. However, the truth is that this inner resistance is not an enemy. It is a part of you. It's a part that's holding a lot of suffering and believes it's protecting you.

MODULAR CONSTRUCTIVISM: THE MIND AS A COMMUNITY OF PARTS

The theory of *modular constructivism* can help us get a clearer picture of how these parts operate. The mind is not one unified self. It's more like a community, made up of many different parts. Each part holds its own memories, beliefs, strategies, and emotional tones. At different times, different parts become active, and we experience life through their lens.

It's like the movie *Inside Out*, except your parts are not separate emotions. They are unique to your life. There might be a part of me that loves animals, and it's made out of all my positive experiences with animals. When I'm around a friendly dog, that part comes online. I might have another part that believes I'm never fully safe, and it's made out of my childhood trauma. If the dog starts growling, that part comes online instead.

Most of the time this system works well. A part that knows how to be playful shows up when we're with a child. A part that knows how to focus and analyze comes online when we're solving a problem. A part that carries sadness appears when we're grieving. The self is constructed moment by moment from whichever parts are activated.

Trouble arises when parts come into conflict. One part of you wants to grow, while another part holds back. One longs for intimacy; another fears it. The push and pull between parts creates the felt sense of ambivalence: of wanting and not wanting at the same time. Depression often thrives in this gap.

KEGAN AND LAHEY'S COMPETING COMMITMENTS

Authors Robert Kegan and Lisa Lahey call this kind of inner conflict a *competing commitment*. On the surface, we have a conscious goal: *I want to practice self-compassion, I want to get better, I want to be free of depression*. Beneath the surface, another part carries a hidden commitment: *If I stop criticizing myself, I'll lose all motivation. If I open up to others, I'll be hurt again. If I let myself feel joy, it will only be taken away.*

Both commitments are real. The surface commitment represents your conscious aspiration. The competing commitment represents an unconscious part trying to protect you. These two run in parallel, like different programs on a computer, creating inner resistance and paralysis.

THE BUDDHIST FRAME: HABIT ENERGIES AND LATENT TENDENCIES

Buddhist psychology describes this same phenomenon in its own language. In the early teachings, these protective parts are called *anusaya*, latent tendencies that lie dormant until conditions awaken them. Each *anusaya* is tied to a protective view (*diṭṭhi*), often centered on identity: *I am only safe if I stay small; I will only be loved if I succeed; I am worthless unless I keep striving.* When life touches a raw place, the latent tendency springs to life, producing clinging (*upādāna*) and defensive reactions (*saṅkhāra*) that override your stated intention.

Later *Mahāyāna* Buddhism uses the term *vāsanā*, or "habit energy." These are the seeds (*bīja*) stored deep in consciousness, perfumed by past experience. When the conditions ripen, they sprout as patterns of thought, feeling, and action. In Tibet, this is often called *shenpa*, that hooked, automatic tightening around an old identity-protecting story.

However we name it—*anusaya*, *vāsanā*, competing commitment, or protective part—the dynamic is the same. A part of you longs for freedom, and another part clings to strategies born of old suffering.

PARALLEL PROCESSING AND AMBIVALENCE

One of the important insights from all of these traditions is that these parts don't take turns in a neat sequence. They run in *parallel processing*. That means you can have two contradictory commitments active at once. One part of you may be trying to move toward healing, while another is simultaneously pulling you back into the familiar place of despair. The experience of ambivalence, of wanting change and resisting it at the same time, is not evidence of failure. It is simply what happens when conflicting parts of the self are activated together.

REFRAMING RESISTANCE

Understanding resistance in this way helps us reframe it. Resistance is not laziness. It is not self-sabotage. It is not proof that you can't heal. Resistance is a form of protection. It is a part of you, carrying old wounds and trying to keep you safe the only way it knows how.

The purpose of this section is to help you get to know these parts of yourself, understand the hidden commitments that drive them, and learn how to meet them with compassion. When you can hear the suffering at the core of a competing commitment, you can begin to transform it. The part that once resisted healing can become an ally, offering energy and insight that supports your growth.

In the chapters ahead, we explore how competing commitments show up in depression, how to recognize your own, and how to transform them at their roots. By learning to listen to the voices of resistance with compassion, you may find that what once blocked you becomes the very path forward.

33

HOW COMPETING COMMITMENTS SHOW UP IN DEPRESSION

On the surface, competing commitments look like self-sabotage. They look like avoiding our practice, dismissing encouragement, or clinging to criticism. When we look deeper, each one makes its own kind of sense.

In this chapter, I share some examples of how competing commitments often manifest in depression. As you read, notice if any of these feel familiar. You may recognize yourself in one of these stories, or in all of them.

DIRECT VERSUS INDIRECT COMPETING COMMITMENTS

Not all competing commitments operate in the same way. Some are *direct*. They are parts of us that explicitly want to *maintain depression* because they believe it's safer or the only way to get our needs met. Others are *indirect*. These are parts that are attached to strategies like self-criticism, avoidance, or perfectionism, which create depression as a by-product.

Understanding this distinction can help us recognize the different "flavors" of resistance and meet them more precisely.

DIRECT COMPETING COMMITMENTS

These are parts that explicitly *want* you to stay depressed, because depression itself feels important.

Examples

- *Safety through collapse.* Olivia grew up in a family where any expression of confidence or joy was met with ridicule. As an adult, part of her believes the only way to be safe is to stay small and collapsed. For this part, depression is a shield against attack.

- *Love through helplessness.* Marcus discovered as a child that the only time he received warmth from his parents was when he was sick or struggling. A part of him learned *If I'm weak and dependent, people will care about me.* His depression keeps him in that role, hoping for attention and comfort.

- *Avoiding responsibility.* Deep down, Sarah fears she is incapable of succeeding. For one part of her, depression functions as an excuse: *If I'm depressed, I won't have to face the risk of trying and failing.* This part is directly invested in maintaining her depression as a way of avoiding humiliation.

- *Punishment as control.* James grew up believing he was bad and deserved to suffer. A part of him clings to depression as a kind of penance—better to punish himself than to wait for others to punish him. This direct commitment holds on to depression itself as a form of safety.

INDIRECT COMPETING COMMITMENTS

These are parts that don't want depression itself, but cling to strategies that *cause* or *reinforce* depression.

Examples

- *Self-criticism as motivation.* Lena is terrified that if she stops criticizing herself, she'll become lazy or a failure. Her competing commitment is to hold on to self-attack as fuel. The unintended consequence is depression.
- *Perfectionism as protection.* Alex's part insists he must always be perfect to avoid shame. That constant pressure leaves him anxious, depleted, and depressed. The goal is to prevent shame, but the side effect is despair.
- *Avoidance of vulnerability.* Grace feels a deep longing for closeness, but another part avoids intimacy at all costs.

Its commitment is to protect her from rejection. The unintended cost is loneliness and depression.

- *Hopelessness as protection against disappointment.* Ravi is afraid to hope. A part of him says, "If I expect things to improve, I'll only be crushed when they don't." So he stays in despair. The commitment is to avoid disappointment, but it leaves him trapped in depression.

THE PARADOX OF PROTECTION

In each of these examples, the competing commitment is not irrational. It's painful, yes, but it is also trying to serve a purpose. The critic wants to keep us safe from failure. The fear of joy wants to spare us heartbreak. Perfectionism shields us from shame. Isolation protects us from betrayal. Despair guards us from the devastation of broken hope.

This is why resistance is such a powerful force in depression. It's not just stubbornness or laziness. It is a part of the mind clinging to an old survival strategy. What once helped us cope has now become a prison.

WHY THE DISTINCTION MATTERS

When we understand whether a part is holding on to depression *directly* or clinging to a protective strategy *indirectly*, we know where to aim our compassion:

- With *direct commitments*, the work is to show the part that it no longer needs depression to be safe or loved.
- With *indirect commitments*, the work is to acknowledge the protective strategy, and then gently explore how it creates more suffering than it prevents.

Both kinds of commitments are born from suffering. Both can be transformed through awareness and compassion.

TURNING TOWARD THE PROTECTORS

The good news is that once we recognize competing commitments for what they are, we can begin to work with them. Instead of trying to fight or suppress resistance, we can turn toward these protectors with compassion.

Later chapters guide you step-by-step through that process: how to recognize resistance in your own life, how to uncover the hidden commitment behind it, and how to transform the suffering at its core.

For now, the most important thing to remember is this: Resistance makes sense. The parts of you that hold back are not your enemies. They are protectors carrying old pain. By learning to listen to them, you are already beginning the work of transformation.

34

NOTICING RESISTANCE WITHOUT BLAME

If you've ever told yourself "I know this practice could help, but I just can't make myself do it," you're not alone. Every reader who makes it this far in the book has felt that same tension. You might even be feeling it right now.

The key is this: Resistance isn't laziness, weakness, or failure. It's not a sign that something is wrong with you. Resistance is simply a signal that a competing commitment has been activated.

THE FIRST STEP: NAMING RESISTANCE

Most of us are so used to blaming ourselves that the first step can feel radical. Instead of asking, "What's wrong with me?" try asking, "What part of me is protecting me right now?"

When you notice yourself procrastinating, avoiding your practice, or dismissing it as useless, pause. Name what is happening as "resistance." Just that word helps shift you out of judgment and into curiosity. *This is resistance. That means a part of me is trying to protect me.*

That simple reframe creates space. It turns a moment of shame into a moment of listening.

COMMON SIGNS OF RESISTANCE

Resistance doesn't always announce itself loudly. Sometimes it looks like:

- *Procrastination*—I'll do it later.
- *Numbing*—Scrolling, overeating, zoning out.
- *Dismissal*—This is stupid. It won't work.
- *Perfectionism*—I have to get it exactly right, so I can't even start.
- *Avoidance*—Suddenly remembering a thousand other "urgent" tasks.
- *Skepticism*—This might work for other people, but not for me.

Each of these is a protective part stepping in.

A GENTLE INQUIRY

When you catch resistance, try a gentle inquiry instead of blame. You might ask yourself:

- "If this practice worked, what might go wrong?"
- "What would I have to risk if I followed through?"
- "What bad outcome is this part of me afraid of?"

These questions don't need to be answered right away. Simply holding them with curiosity can begin to soften the grip of resistance.

SELF-COMPASSION IN THE MOMENT

It's easy to feel frustrated when you notice resistance, but what that part of you needs most is kindness. You might try placing a hand on your heart and saying quietly:

- "It makes sense that I feel resistance. This part wants to protect me."
- "Thank you for wanting to keep me safe."

This is not about giving in to resistance. It's about creating the conditions to understand it. When a protector part feels heard, it can begin to relax.

PRACTICE: JOURNALING WITH RESISTANCE

Here's a simple practice you can try:

1. Set aside 5 minutes with a pen and paper.
2. Choose a practice from Section II that you avoided or dismissed, and read it again.
3. Write down exactly what your resistance says. Examples:
   - "This is stupid and it will never work."
   - "If I allow joy, I'll only get hurt."
   - "If I open up, people will betray me."
4. When you're done, put your hand on your heart and read your list back gently, as if you were listening to a friend.

This exercise helps bring the competing commitment into the light, where it can be met with compassion instead of shame.

THE TURNING POINT

The simple act of noticing resistance without blame is a turning point. Instead of battling yourself, you begin to listen. Instead of seeing resistance as failure, you see it as a protector carrying old pain. This shift in perspective prepares the ground for the next step: learning how to explore your own competing commitment in more depth, and uncovering the suffering at its core.

35

EXPLORING YOUR OWN COMPETING COMMITMENTS

By now, we've seen that resistance is not the enemy. It is a part that's trying to protect us. We've also named some of the most common competing commitments in depression—both direct and indirect. Now you're ready to recognize and explore *your own* competing commitments.

This chapter guides you through that process. The goal is not to defeat resistance, but to listen to it and heal it. When you can meet your own protectors with curiosity and compassion, they begin to soften, and you can uncover the suffering at their core.

WHY COMPASSION SOMETIMES FEELS IMPOSSIBLE

Many people come to self-compassion practice expecting it to feel soothing right away. But sometimes, instead of comfort, what arises is resistance. For some, kindness toward themselves feels fake. For others, it feels dangerous. Instead of softening, they tighten. Instead of relief, they feel a wave of unease or even anger.

When this happens, it doesn't mean you're doing the practice wrong. It means you've touched something important. A part of you is stepping in to say, "This isn't safe." That part may believe that self-criticism is the only thing keeping you motivated, or that if you let yourself feel cared for, you'll become vulnerable and be hurt.

If compassion feels impossible, there might be a hidden part of you that's protecting an old wound. In fact, the moment when compassion feels hardest is often the very moment you've arrived at the doorway of deep change.

Step 1: Notice What Feels Wrong

Think of a moment when you tried one of the practices earlier in this book and felt resistance. Maybe you thought, "This is pointless," or you found yourself distracted, numb, or angry.

Instead of pushing past that feeling, pause. Ask yourself:

- "What feels wrong about this practice?"
- "What am I afraid would happen if I allowed it to work?"

Sometimes the answer comes as a thought. Other times it's just a vague unease. Whatever comes, trust it. Write it down, even if it doesn't make sense yet.

Step 2: Imagine the Protector's Perspective

Once you've named what feels wrong, imagine that resistance as a part of you—a protector with its own perspective.

Ask gently:

- "What is your job?"
- "What are you afraid will happen if I change?"
- "What are you trying to protect me from?"

For example:

- If you resist letting go of self-criticism, the protector may say, "Without me, you'll fail and be humiliated."
- If you resist joy, the protector may say, "If you get happy, it will be ripped away, and you won't survive the loss."
- If you resist connection, the protector may say, "If you get close to people, they'll hurt you again."

Even when the logic feels twisted, there is always suffering at the core.

Step 3: Hold the Resistance With Compassion

Now, place a hand on your heart and acknowledge this part of you directly:

- "I see how hard you've been working to keep me safe."

- "It makes sense that you would be afraid of this change."
- "Thank you for trying to protect me. I will listen to you."

You are not promising to obey that part forever. You are simply recognizing the pain behind it. When a protector feels heard, it often begins to soften. You are playing the part of the peacemaker.

Step 4: Trace the Commitment

Every competing commitment is built around a kind of hidden contract: *I must do this, or else something terrible will happen.*

Try completing one of these sentences:

- "If I stop criticizing myself . . . "
- "If I allow myself to feel joy . . . "
- "If I reach out for connection . . . "
- "If I let go of depression . . . "
- "If I let myself hope . . . "

Keep going until you find the fear underneath. That fear is the heart of the competing commitment.

Step 5: Stay Curious

This process can bring up strong emotions, such as fear, anger, grief. If you start to feel overwhelmed, pause. Go back to a grounding practice, like mindful breathing or feeling your feet on the floor.

Remind yourself: *This is just a part of me. I don't have to believe it completely. I just need to listen.*

A PRACTICE TO TRY: DIALOGUING WITH RESISTANCE

Here's a journaling exercise:

1. Write down a self-compassion phrase, like *May I be kind to myself.*
2. Notice any resistance that arises. Write down what it says, exactly as you hear it:
   - "That's pathetic."
   - "You don't deserve kindness."
   - "If you soften, you'll fail."

1. Now write a compassionate response back to the resistant voice:
   - "I hear that you're scared I'll fail if I'm kind to myself."
   - "You've been trying to keep me safe by being hard on me."
   - "Thank you for protecting me. Can we try a different way together?"

Go back and forth for a few rounds. See what shifts.

MOVING FORWARD

Exploring competing commitments can be tender work. You may uncover old beliefs or painful memories. Remember: The goal is not to dismantle everything at once. The goal is to begin listening so that resistance becomes an entry point to healing rather than a wall.

In the next chapter, we look at the most common competing commitments in depression, and how to recognize them in your own life.

36

COMMON COMPETING COMMITMENTS IN DEPRESSION

By now, you've seen how competing commitments show up in real life: One part of you longs for change, while another part quietly pulls in the opposite direction. This chapter steps back from individual stories to create a map.

Here we look at some of the most common competing commitments in depression. Think of them as recurring patterns. You may see yourself in one or several. Hopefully this presentation will help you understand your own competing commitments more fully.

Each commitment follows a similar shape:

- There is something you consciously long for.
- There is a hidden contract that says pursuing it would be unsafe.

INDIRECT COMPETING COMMITMENTS

These don't want depression itself but cling to strategies that indirectly keep depression in place.

1. Maintaining Connection

- *Surface commitment*: "I want to recognize that I never deserved to be abused."
- *Competing commitment*: "If I realize that, then my parents become horrible people. If I deserved the abuse, I can continue feeling connected with them."
- *Protective view*: Believing I deserved it preserves a sense of belonging.
- *Unintended effect*: Staying identified with blame prevents full healing and keeps me tied to painful bonds.

2. Maintaining the Illusion of Control

- *Surface commitment*: "I want to let go of blaming myself."
- *Competing commitment*: "If I'm to blame, then I can control it by becoming better. If I'm not to blame, then it's entirely outside of my control—and that is scary."
- *Protective view*: Self-blame creates the illusion that I can prevent harm.

- *Unintended effect*: The cycle of self-blame deepens depression and erodes self-worth.

3. Maintaining Fairness

- *Surface commitment*: "I want to see clearly that I didn't deserve what happened."
- *Competing commitment*: "If I'm not to blame, then I live in a world where good people can be hurt for no reason. That would feel too unfair."
- *Protective view*: Believing I caused it makes the world feel more just.
- *Unintended effect*: The sense of fairness is maintained at the cost of ongoing self-condemnation.

4. Protecting a Relationship

- *Surface commitment*: "I want to believe I am lovable."
- *Competing commitment*: "If I believe I'm lovable, someone important in my life will reject me."
- *Protective view*: Staying unlovable keeps a fragile relationship intact.
- *Unintended effect*: My own healing feels like a threat to attachment, so I keep myself small.

5. Avoiding Responsibility

   - *Surface commitment*: "I want to see that there's nothing wrong with me."
   - *Competing commitment*: "If I know I'm not broken, then I become responsible for my life. Believing I'm broken lets me escape responsibility."
   - *Protective view*: Defectiveness offers a shield from accountability.
   - *Unintended effect*: Growth stalls because responsibility feels unsafe.

6. Avoiding Hope

   - *Surface commitment*: "I want to believe things could get better."
   - *Competing commitment*: "If I let myself hope, I'll be crushed if it doesn't work out."
   - *Protective view*: Hopelessness prevents disappointment.
   - *Unintended effect*: Depression is sustained as a defense against heartbreak.

7. Avoiding Grief

- *Surface commitment*: "I want to accept that I didn't deserve what happened."
- *Competing commitment*: "If I accept that, I'll have to feel the grief of what was taken from me."
- *Protective view*: Self-blame is easier than mourning the loss.
- *Unintended effect*: Grief is avoided, but the wound remains unhealed.

8. Avoiding Vulnerability

- *Surface commitment*: "I want to allow myself to be open."
- *Competing commitment*: "If I let myself be open, I'll get hurt again."
- *Protective view*: Avoidance of vulnerability prevents further harm.
- *Unintended effect*: Intimacy and connection are blocked, reinforcing isolation.

9. Maintaining Loyalty

- *Surface commitment*: "I want to grow and heal."
- *Competing commitment*: "If I grow, it will feel like I'm betraying my family."
- *Protective view*: Staying in pain preserves loyalty to those who suffered before me.
- *Unintended effect*: My loyalty keeps me tied to cycles of suffering that could otherwise be transformed.

10. Maintaining Identity

- *Surface commitment*: "I want to let go of my suffering."
- *Competing commitment*: "If I stop suffering, I won't know who I am anymore."
- *Protective view*: Suffering has become part of my identity, and losing it feels like losing myself.
- *Unintended effect*: Healing is resisted to preserve a familiar sense of self, even when it's painful.

11. Self-Criticism as Motivation

- *Surface commitment*: "I want to treat myself with kindness."

- *Competing commitment*: "If I stop criticizing myself, I'll collapse."
- *Protective view*: Self-attack is the only thing keeping me motivated.
- *Unintended effect*: The inner critic erodes confidence, feeding hopelessness and despair.

12. Punishment as Control

- *Surface commitment*: "I want to forgive myself and move forward."
- *Competing commitment*: "If I stop punishing myself, I'll be letting myself off the hook."
- *Protective view*: Constant self-punishment keeps me from repeating mistakes.
- *Unintended effect*: Depression deepens as life becomes dominated by shame.

13. Fear of Weakness

- *Surface commitment*: "I want to be gentle with myself."
- *Competing commitment*: "If I show myself compassion, it means I'm weak, selfish, or indulgent."
- *Protective view*: Toughness is the only way to survive.

- *Unintended effect*: Attempts at kindness feel dangerous, leaving the cycle of harshness intact.

14. Acceptance Equals Stagnation

- *Surface commitment*: "I want to accept myself as I am."
- *Competing commitment*: "If I accept myself, I'll never change."
- *Protective view*: Self-criticism and dissatisfaction are the only paths to improvement.
- *Unintended effect*: Growth stalls under the weight of constant self-rejection.

15. Perfectionism as Protection

- *Surface commitment*: "I want to rest and feel enough as I am."
- *Competing commitment*: "If I let my guard down, I'll be exposed and humiliated."
- *Protective view*: Flawlessness is the only shield against shame.
- *Unintended effect*: Exhaustion and emptiness create fertile ground for depression.

16. Fear of Joy

- *Surface commitment*: "I want to feel happiness again."
- *Competing commitment*: "If I allow joy, it will be taken away—and that pain will be unbearable."
- *Protective view*: Better to stay numb than risk heartbreak.
- *Unintended effect*: Depression thrives in the absence of joy.

17. Isolation as Safety

- *Surface commitment*: "I want deeper connection with others."
- *Competing commitment*: "If I let people close, they'll hurt me."
- *Protective view*: Vulnerability equals danger.
- *Unintended effect*: Loneliness and disconnection reinforce depression.

18. Despair as Protection Against Disappointment

- *Surface commitment*: "I want to believe things can change."
- *Competing commitment*: "If I let myself hope, I'll be crushed when it doesn't work out."

- *Protective view*: Staying hopeless prevents heartbreak.
- *Unintended effect*: Depression is maintained as a defense against hope.

DIRECT COMPETING COMMITMENTS

These are parts that actually *want* you to stay depressed, because depression itself feels like the safest option.

19. Depression as Connection

- *Surface commitment*: "I want to be well."
- *Competing commitment*: "If I collapse, maybe someone will finally notice and care."
- *Protective view*: Suffering is the only way to be loved or attended to.
- *Unintended effect*: Depression becomes a strategy for belonging.

20. Depression as Penance

- *Surface commitment*: "I want relief."
- *Competing commitment*: "I deserve to suffer for who I am or what I've done."

- *Protective view*: Self-inflicted suffering will prevent worse punishment from others.
- *Unintended effect*: Pain is prolonged and compassion feels forbidden.

USING THIS MAP

You may find that one or two of these stand out right away. Others may feel unfamiliar, but ring true when you sit with them. The point isn't to identify the "right" one, but to notice how resistance in depression almost always has a protective logic.

Every one of these commitments is a survival strategy. They are not evidence that you are broken. They are parts of you doing the best they can to shield you from danger, shame, or heartbreak.

In the chapters ahead, we trace these commitments back to the suffering at their core. When we can meet that suffering with compassion, the result is transformation at the base.

37

TRACING RESISTANCE TO ITS CORE OF SUFFERING

When resistance arises, it often feels like we've hit a wall. We try to practice self-compassion or to reach for joy, and something inside says "No." At first, this can feel like sabotage, as if part of us is determined to keep us stuck. But if we look closely, every competing commitment is organized around an old wound. Beneath the strategy, whether it's self-criticism, avoidance, despair, or depression itself, there is always pain.

In Buddhist terms, these patterns are latent tendencies (*anusaya*) tied to protective views (*diṭṭhi*). When triggered, they produce clinging (*upādāna*) and defensive reactions (*saṅkhāra*). In *Mahāyāna* language, they are habit energies (*vāsanā*) or karmic seeds (*bīja*) stored in consciousness, waiting for conditions to ripen. In everyday language: They are inner parts of us, carrying painful experiences that hardened into worldviews, and strategies meant to protect us from being hurt again.

FROM EXPERIENCE TO WORLDVIEW

Each inner part has its own history. At some point, something happened. It could have been humiliation, abandonment, betrayal, or loss. Whatever it was, it was too much to bear. Out of that pain, the part formed a worldview (*diṭṭhi*):

- "The only way to be safe is to stay small."
- "I will only be loved if I'm suffering."
- "If I stop criticizing myself, I'll collapse."
- "Joy is dangerous because it will be taken away."

Once a worldview has formed, it drives a *protective strategy*. Collapse becomes a shield. Self-criticism becomes armor. Numbness becomes a refuge. Each strategy "works" in the sense that it prevents the unbearable from happening again. Yet over time, the strategy itself creates more suffering.

UNDERSTANDING AS LOVE

Thich Nhat Hanh taught that "understanding is love." When we encounter a competing commitment, the first task is not to change it, but to understand it. We must listen deeply to how its worldview was made out of the experiences it carries, and how that worldview gave rise to its protective strategy.

When we understand, compassion naturally follows. We can see that this part is not our enemy but merely doing its best with the information it has. As soon as we see it that way, tenderness arises.

FROM STRATEGY BACK TO SUFFERING

Tracing resistance to its core means following the thread backward:

- From strategy to worldview.
  - "I avoid joy." → "Joy is dangerous."
  - "I criticize myself." → "If I stop, I'll be worthless."

- From worldview to experience.
  - "Joy is dangerous" → remembering the moment when happiness was followed by devastating loss.
  - "If I stop criticizing myself, I'll be worthless" → recalling how only achievement earned attention or love.

At the center, we find suffering: shame, fear, grief, abandonment. Each part is made of those painful experiences. It is carrying them for us, and trying to prevent them from happening again.

MEETING THE PART WITH COMPASSION

When you encounter resistance, pause. Instead of pushing through, imagine turning toward the part with gentleness. You might place a hand on your heart and say:

- "I see how hard you've worked to protect me."

- "I understand why you believe this strategy is necessary."
- "Thank you for carrying this pain for me. I will listen."

This simple act of recognition can be profoundly healing. The part feels less alone, less condemned. And you, the larger self, begin to embody compassion.

SHARING MISSING INFORMATION

Once a protector part feels understood, it may be open to new information. Many of these parts are operating with outdated worldviews, formed in childhood or moments of trauma. They don't know that circumstances have changed.

For example:

- The critic doesn't know you now have other sources of motivation.
- The fearful part doesn't know that joy can be safe when shared with supportive people.
- The isolated part doesn't know that healthy boundaries can protect you in relationships.

We can gently share this information, not by lecturing the part but by showing it through experience. We offer compassion, practicing joy in small doses, testing connection in safe contexts. In this way, the worldview begins to expand, and the protective strategy is no longer needed.

PRACTICE: TRACING THE THREAD

1. *Notice the resistance.* Pause when you catch yourself avoiding or dismissing a practice.
2. *Ask what feels wrong.* Invite the part to voice its worldview: "If I let this practice work, what bad thing might happen?"
3. *Listen for the suffering.* Sense the pain underneath the worldview. Is it shame? Fear? Loss?
4. *Acknowledge and thank.* Place a hand on your heart: "I see the pain you carry, and I understand why you protect me this way. Thank you."
5. *Gently offer new possibilities.* Share with the part, in words or action: "I'm not that powerless child anymore. Joy can be safe. Connection can be chosen."

Every part that resists healing is made of past suffering. Each carries its own worldview and protective strategy. When we trace resistance back to its core, we see not an obstacle but a protector and the wound it is guarding.

Understanding is love. When we understand how a part was

shaped by pain, compassion flows naturally. And when compassion touches that wound, the worldview can expand, the strategy can relax, and the path to healing opens.

38

MEETING THE PROTECTOR WITH COMPASSION

In the previous chapter, we traced resistance back to its source. Beneath every competing commitment is an inner protector—a part of us shaped by pain, carrying a worldview that was true enough at the time. These protectors learned that collapse keeps us safe, self-hatred is the only way to stay good, or joy is too dangerous to touch. They're the product of some painful experience that needs healing.

This chapter is about how to meet those protectors. Not with strategy, but with compassion.

WHEN YOU SEE THE LOGIC, LOVE BECOMES POSSIBLE

Often, the moment we understand a protector's logic, something softens. The part stops feeling like an obstacle and starts feeling like someone you know. Someone who's been guarding a doorway, exhausted and alone, waiting for help to come. When we recognize what the part has been trying to protect us from, and how much of its life has been spent doing that job, we stop trying to fight it. We want to care for it.

That's the shift we're looking for.

Compassion doesn't mean you want that part to continue what it's been doing. It means you stop treating it like the enemy. You stop trying to control or suppress it. Instead, you show up like you would for a frightened child. You sit down beside it and say, "I see you. You don't have to do this alone."

HOW TO BE WITH A PROTECTOR

The first step is recognizing that this part of you isn't bad. It's limited. It was shaped by specific experiences and locked into a narrow worldview: *It's not safe to relax. You don't deserve kindness. You have to stay small to survive.*

The practice is not to argue with the part, but to accompany it. Not to explain its logic away, but to let it be seen.

You might say something like:

- "I understand why you believe that."
- "That makes so much sense."
- "You've been working so hard for so long."

That might sound strange at first. But remember: This isn't performance. It's not a trick. This is your real relationship with a real part of you. Like any relationship, it changes when there's warmth, honesty, and when someone finally listens.

WHAT THE PROTECTOR MIGHT SAY

If you ask gently, "What are you afraid would happen if I changed?" You might hear something like:

- "If you stop blaming yourself, you'll feel how unfair it was."
- "If you let go of depression, you'll be expected to do more than you can handle."
- "If you allow joy, you'll be crushed when it disappears again."

Even if the answer feels irrational, don't dismiss it. It's only irrational if you forget what this part has lived through.

This is why we don't try to force change. We seek to understand the suffering at the root of our issue, and send it compassion.

UPDATING THE WORLDVIEW

Once a part feels seen, it can become more open. It might be willing to hear something new.

You don't have to convince it. Just offer a gentle truth:

- "You don't have to collapse to be loved."
- "I know more now. I have choices I didn't have before."
- "You're not alone anymore."

Some protectors won't be ready to hear that. That's okay. You're not there to win them over. You're there to stay with them, no matter how long it takes.

PRACTICE: A COMPASSIONATE MEETING

1. Settle

Find a quiet place to sit or lie down. Let your body rest in a way that feels safe. Follow the sensation of your breath.

2. Invite the Protector

Think of a moment when you felt stuck, ashamed, or deeply resistant to change. See if you can feel where that resistance lives in your body. Let it know you're listening.

3. Listen

Ask inwardly: "What are you afraid would happen if I let this go?" Don't force an answer. Just wait. If nothing comes, that's okay. You've already made contact.

4. Reflect

If you do hear something, such as a thought, a feeling, or a memory, acknowledge it.

Say: "That makes sense" or "Thanks for letting me know."

5. Offer Care

Place a hand on your heart or wherever the protector seems to live.

Say: "You've done so much. Thank you." You might add: "You don't have to do this job forever. I can help."

6. Offer a New Possibility

Only if it feels welcome, say something new:

"It's different now."

"We're safe here."

"You're allowed to rest."

7. Rest Together

Breathe with the part. Let it be there, exactly as it is. Don't try to finish anything. Just stay.

THE PROTECTOR CHANGES WHEN IT'S NO LONGER ALONE

These parts don't change because we convince them. They change when the pain they carry is finally met with compassion or when the rigid worldview they've been holding gets updated with new information. Either way, it's not a battle. It's a process of dialogue and empathy.

Some protectors soften as soon as they feel understood. Others need time. What matters most is that you're willing to stay with them. Not to fix or negotiate, but to bear witness. To say, "I see you. I know why you've been doing this."

Your job isn't to rush the process. Your job is to offer what this part has never had: your presence, your curiosity, your care. That's what allows healing to begin.

39

HEALING YOUR COMPETING COMMITMENT

Up to this point, we've learned how to recognize competing commitments, distinguish direct and indirect forms, and meet the protector parts with compassion. Now we focus directly on healing the suffering from the past that these parts embody.

Each competing commitment is built around painful experiences that hardened into a worldview (*diṭṭhi*). From that worldview, a protective strategy formed. To truly transform resistance, the suffering at the core of that part needs healing.

This chapter guides you in how to bring compassion and mindfulness directly to those wounds.

THE CRYING CHILD WITHIN

When Thich Nhat Hanh taught about suffering, he often compared it to a crying child. If you try to ignore the child or scold them for crying, the suffering only grows stronger. The only thing that helps is to pick the child up, hold them, and listen.

The same is true for our inner protectors. Each competing commitment is like a child carrying unbearable pain. Its strategy—criticism, collapse, isolation, or numbness—is its way of surviving. Healing means holding the suffering with compassion and offering it new conditions so it no longer needs to cry alone.

Step 1: Contacting the Experience

Every competing commitment is rooted in a part that embodies painful experiences. Healing begins by contacting the embodied sense of that pain.

When you notice resistance, pause and ask:

- "Where do I feel this in my body?"
- "What sensations are here—tightness, heaviness, trembling, numbness?"
- "What feeling is this part carrying—shame, fear, grief, loneliness?"

You don't need to recall every detail of the original memory. The body remembers. The sensations themselves are the doorway.

Take a few mindful breaths and simply acknowledge: *This is the suffering my protector carries.*

Step 2: Holding With Loving-Awareness

Once the suffering is contacted, the next step is to hold it in loving-awareness.

Place a hand gently on your heart or wherever you feel the

sensation most strongly. Breathe slowly. Imagine that you are holding a crying child with tenderness, patience, and presence.

Say inwardly:

- "I see your pain."
- "I understand why you protect me."
- "I am here with you."

This is the heart of the practice. Understanding the suffering is itself love. The protector begins to soften because it feels seen.

Step 3: Seeing the Worldview

Every competing commitment rests on a worldview (*diṭṭhi*). Out of painful experiences, the part came to believe:

- The only way to stay safe is to collapse.
- I will only be loved if I am suffering.
- If I stop criticizing myself, I will fail.
- Joy is dangerous because it will be taken away.

When you listen to the suffering, see if you can also notice the worldview it carries. Don't argue with it or try to correct it right away. Just recognize: *This is how this part sees the world based on the pain it carries.*

Step 4: Offering Compassion and New Conditions

Once the suffering has been acknowledged and the worldview recognized, you can gently offer new conditions. Many protectors are operating with outdated information: worldviews formed in childhood or moments of trauma. They don't know that life has changed.

You might say inwardly:

- "I know you learned that joy is dangerous, but we have safety now."
- "You believed criticism was the only way to keep us moving, but I can find other sources of motivation."
- "You thought collapse was the only way to get love, but there are healthier ways to connect now."

This isn't about forcing a new belief. It's about sharing information that allows the worldview to expand. In Buddhist terms, you are watering new seeds (*bīja*) in consciousness, while soothing the old habit energy (*vāsanā*) with compassion.

PRACTICE: HEALING THE PROTECTOR

Here is a practice you can try:

1. *Settle.* Sit comfortably. Breathe gently. Place a hand on your heart.

2. *Invite the protector.* Recall a moment of resistance. Let the part that resists come forward. Notice where you feel it in your body.

3. *Contact the suffering.* Ask: "What pain are you carrying?" Allow the sensation to arise in your body.

4. *Hold with compassion.* Breathe with the part. Say: "I see your pain. I understand why you protect me. I am here with you."

5. *Recognize the worldview.* Listen for the belief the part holds. "Joy is dangerous. Self-criticism keeps me safe. Collapse is the only way to get love."

6. *Offer new conditions.* Gently share an update: "It's different now. We have strength and support. There are other ways to be safe."

7. *Rest.* Sit quietly with the part, letting compassion and new understanding settle in.

WHY THIS HEALS

When suffering is met with compassion, it transforms. The latent tendency (*anusaya*) weakens. The worldview (*diṭṭhi*) expands. The protective strategy is no longer necessary.

This is how competing commitments are healed: not by fighting

ORPHAN HOLD
DO NOT SHIP

H1 – 000000000406

ISBN 9781324082453

CLIENT	Alternate Sourcing
STATION	TPP Receiving Station 03
HELD	2026 – 10 – 08 14:18

SHELF

If its order arrives, scan this label at a receiving station.

them but by loving them. Not by rejecting them but by listening to the pain they carry.

Each competing commitment is made of painful experiences that crystallized into a worldview and a strategy. When we contact those experiences, hold them with compassion, and gently offer new conditions, healing unfolds.

By understanding the suffering that formed our competing commitments, we touch them with love. In that love, what once resisted healing can become part of the healing itself.

40

ENCOURAGING WORDS

If you're reading this, I want to begin by saying, "Thank you." Thank you for showing up, again and again, especially when it was hard.

Whether you moved through this book page by page or skipped around looking for something that spoke to what you were feeling, you've come to this moment and I'm grateful you're here.

This isn't the end of a book. It's the continuation of a practice.

THE REAL WORK BEGINS AFTER THE BOOK

Depression can feel like being exiled from your own life, as though there's a wall between you and the present moment, between you and everyone else, even between you and yourself. What this book has been trying to show you is that the wall isn't as solid as it seems. You can learn to come home again.

Maybe not all at once, but one breath, one moment, and one small act of kindness at a time.

LET THIS BE A BOOK YOU LIVE WITH

There's a reason this book is made of short sections. When you're hurting, you need things you can actually reach.

Section II, the heart of this book, was written to be lived with. Keep it close. Don't treat it like something you read and put away. Let it help you through each day and keep you practicing.

You might find one chapter that feels like an anchor for a week or a month. You might flip to a random page and find exactly what you needed. You don't have to follow a schedule. Just keep returning.

Practice doesn't mean doing something perfectly. It means making something your path.

WHAT YOU PRACTICE, YOU STRENGTHEN

In Buddhist psychology, the mind is like a garden. Whatever we water will grow. If we keep practicing compassion, even clumsily, the seeds of compassion grow stronger. If we keep practicing presence, even for just one breath at a time, the seed of presence grows stronger. Even when you feel nothing. Even when the voice in your head says it's pointless. If you bring your awareness gently back to the moment, if you offer yourself even the smallest gesture of care, that matters.

There are always setbacks and always resistance. You will forget everything you've learned here and remember it again—that cycle is not a failure. It's the practice.

YOU ARE NOT ALONE

Sometimes when people are depressed, they believe their pain makes them unlovable. That they're the one person for whom healing is impossible.

Please don't believe that voice.

Everything you've faced—shame, fear, numbness, hopelessness—others have faced too. Others are facing it right now. You are not strange. You are not alone. You are not broken.

The parts of you that suffer most are the parts that most need your tenderness. When you can offer even a moment of that tenderness, stop fighting yourself and start listening, you don't just shift your own inner world. You shift the world around you.

A SMALL BLESSING FOR THE PATH

I want to leave you with this:

- May you remember that healing doesn't come from forcing yourself to be better. It comes from befriending what's here now.
- May you know that joy is not something you have to earn. It's something you can learn to notice.
- May you trust that the seeds of compassion, freedom, and aliveness are already within you, waiting to be watered.

There is no version of life where everything is easy and nothing ever hurts. There is a version where you are present, loving, and free.

Even in the depths of suffering, you can place your hand on your heart and say: "I am here. I am listening. I am not giving up on myself."

That is the path.

GLOSSARY

Akiriyā-diṭṭhi—"Wrong view of inaction"; a distorted belief that what we do can't matter; a hopelessness stance that blocks agency.

Anapanasati Sutta—"Mindfulness of Breathing Discourse," the Buddha's step-by-step guide for complete liberation through 16 exercises on the awareness of the breath.

Anusaya—"Latent tendencies"; deep, dormant patterns that spring to life when triggered; implicit memories/preconscious schemas.

Ayoniso manasikāra—"Unwise attention"; paying attention in ways that reinforce suffering; rumination/negative attentional bias.

Bhaddekaratta Sutta—"The Better Way to Live Alone"; a discourse on not living in the past or the future, but fully in the present.

Bhava-taṇhā—Craving for becoming; the drive to be someone or reach a version of self that finally "counts." For example: perfectionistic striving as a condition for self-worth.

Bīja—"Seed"; every mental quality (e.g., joy, anger, calm) exists as a seed that can be watered or not.

Brahmavihāra/Brahmavihāras—The four "divine abodes" of *mettā* (loving-kindness), *karuṭā* (compassion), *muditā* (sympathetic joy), and *upekkhā* (equanimity). They are systematically taught in Chapter IX of the *Visuddhimagga* ("Path of Purification"), a 5th-century meditation manual by Buddhaghosa.

Diṭṭhi—"View" or worldview; the lens that shapes what we see and how we react; core beliefs/meaning making.

Dukkha—Suffering or unsatisfactoriness; the "wobbly wheel" experience when life grinds or grates.

Gāthā—A short mindfulness verse used to anchor attention in daily life (e.g., upon waking).

Karuṇā—Compassion; the wish that suffering be relieved, which is held with steadiness (equanimity).

Metta/Mettā (**Metta Sutta**)—Loving-kindness; wishing well-being for self and others. The "Discourse on Love" is a classic source.

Micchā-diṭṭhi—"Wrong view"; a distorted worldview (e.g., self-blame as "truth").

Muditā—Sympathetic joy; rejoicing in others' happiness.

Saddhā—Confidence/faith, normally rooted in direct experience or willingness to experiment.

Sangha—Community of practice that helps carry us when we can't carry ourselves.

Saṅkhāra/Saṃskāra—Conditioned formations; learned, automatic pattern-making processes, predictive templates, emotional schemas, and action tendencies that organize experience moment by moment. They are neither fixed nor inherent; they arise from neural plasticity and can be reshaped through awareness and new experience.

Satipaṭṭhāna Sutta—"Foundations of Mindfulness Discourse"; the Buddha's guide to liberation through mindfulness of body, feelings, mind, and dharmas/objects of mind.

Shamatha (**Śamatha**)—"Calm abiding"; stopping, resting, and letting body-mind settle; deep parasympathetic reset/mindful rest.

Sukha—Ease or contented happiness; the "smooth wheel" counterpart to *dukkha*.

Upādāna—Clinging/grasping; tightening around identities, views, or outcomes; rigid control strategies that amplify distress.

Upekkhā—Equanimity; balanced openness to the full range of experience.

Vāsanā—Habit energy; residual momentum of past experiences that keeps patterns alive; conditioned tendencies.

Viriyā—Energy, diligence; steady motivation that comes from clarity and meaning.

INDEX

ABOUT THE AUTHOR

Tim Desmond is a psychotherapist, meditation teacher, and Distinguished Faculty Scholar at Antioch University. A longtime student of Zen Master Thich Nhat Hanh, he is the founder of Peer Collective, and cofounder of Morning Sun Mindfulness Center. He lives in Santa Cruz, CA, and teaches Buddhist practices to audiences around the world. His publications include *Self-Compassion in Psychotherapy* (Norton, 2015), *The Self-Compassion Skills Workbook* (Norton, 2017), and *How to Stay Human in a F*cked Up World* (HarperOne, 2019).

ALSO AVAILABLE IN TIM DESMOND'S *BUDDHIST PRACTICES* SERIES

Buddhist Practices for Healing Trauma

"Real and wise." —Jack Kornfield, PhD, author of *After the Ecstasy, the Laundry*

"Desmond's clear, gentle writing style matches his approach to meeting our traumas and past sufferings . . . [H]e encourages readers to nurture the seeds of compassion within us, making healing within reach." —Sharon Salzberg, author of *Lovingkindness* and *Real Life*

ISBN 978-1-324-08247-7 • Paperback • 224 pages • $23.99 US
Visit **wwnorton.com/bpht**

Buddhist Practices for Calming Anxiety and Regulating Your Nervous System

This book draws from a broad range of Buddhist teachings—not just mindfulness, but the deeper tools of insight, compassion, and transformation. For readers who can't sit in silence for hours, these short, pragmatic exercises will help you find peace in a world filled with noise and pressure.

ISBN 978-1-324-08243-9 • Paperback • 224 pages • $23.99 US
Visit **wwnorton.com/bpca**

Also available from Tim Desmond
The Self-Compassion Skills Workbook: A 14-Day Plan to Transform Your Relationship with Yourself

"Self-compassion is an important, personal skill that allows us to live our lives more fully, especially when we suffer, fail, or feel inadequate. With a user-friendly 'Map' and simple guided meditations, this book engages and supports readers on a potentially life-changing journey of self-discovery and self-kindness."

—Christopher Germer, PhD, Faculty, Harvard Medical School, and author of *The Mindful Path to Self-Compassion*

ISBN: 978-0-393-71218-6 • Paperback • 196 pages • $26.99 US
Visit **wwnorton.com/compassionwkb**